# What God Wants You to Know in 2022

Jamie A. Thomas

ISBN 978-1-63844-582-1 (paperback)
ISBN 978-1-63844-583-8 (digital)

Copyright © 2022 by Jamie A. Thomas

All rights reserved. No part of this publication may be reproduced, distributed, or transmitted in any form or by any means, including photocopying, recording, or other electronic or mechanical methods without the prior written permission of the publisher. For permission requests, solicit the publisher via the address below.

Christian Faith Publishing
832 Park Avenue
Meadville, PA 16335
www.christianfaithpublishing.com

Printed in the United States of America

# Contents

Preface: In the Eye of the Storm .......................................5
Introduction..............................................................11
Chapter 1:   A Journey in Genesis: A Miracle in the Desert........52
Chapter 2:   A Journey in the Book of Exodus: In the
                Shadow of Bondage...............................................60
Chapter 3:   A Journey in the Book of Leviticus: A Holy God......66
Chapter 4:   A Journey in the Book of Numbers: Entry Denied...75
Chapter 5:   A Journey in the Book of Deuteronomy:
                Innocent from Murder ..........................................82
Chapter 6:   A Journey in the Book of Joshua:
                An Early Reward ..................................................87
Chapter 7:   A Journey in the Book of Judges: Civil War..............95
Chapter 8:   A Journey in 1 Samuel: A True Friend ...................102
Chapter 9:   A Journey in the Book of 2 Samuel: The
                Wisdom of a Woman ........................................109
Chapter 10: A Journey in the Book of I Kings: Defeating
                the Syrian Empire................................................114
Chapter 11: A Journey in the Book of 2 Kings: A Sign
                from God...........................................................120
Chapter 12: A Journey in the Book of 1 Chronicles:
                Derailing a King..................................................128
Chapter 13: A Journey in 2 Chronicles: Singing on Earth
                and in Heaven....................................................135
Chapter 14: A Journey in the Book of Job:
                The Falsely Accused .............................................143

Chapter 15: A Journey in the Book of Psalms: Exalt His
            Name in Praise ......................................................149
Chapter 16: A Journey in the Book of Proverbs:
            The Substance of Your Inheritance ........................155
Chapter 17: A Journey in the Book of Isaiah: Babylon
            and Arabia............................................................162
Chapter 18: A Journey in the Book of Jeremiah: The Fall
            of Jerusalem..........................................................188
Chapter 19: A Journey in the Book of Ezekiel: In a Nutshell......194
Chapter 20: Five Journeys in the New Testament ......................200

# PREFACE

## In the Eye of the Storm

We all experience storms. Whether we have endured a light rain shower or a category 5 hurricane, we all have them etched in our lives. So it goes for all of humanity, regardless of one's religious faith. However, religious faith always comes to the forefront when death calls, whether it comes slowly or suddenly. This is where faith is truly put to the test.

There was no concern nor question of my faith on August 12, 1996. It was on that day that I was deep under the beautiful hills of West Virginia with eleven other coal miners. It was a normal day in the coal mine until tragedy struck at 11:10 a.m. As I was at the mining face, the four-foot roof supports failed, and the roof suddenly collapsed over my body. In a moment of time, my powerless body was thrust to the mine floor, covering me with over four feet of rock. I'll never forget the sound of all the air within my lungs being forced out by the vast rock crushing me unmercifully to the mine floor. There was little time to react, and the only thought I had was this: I was dead. Period. Every coal miner knows that if you ever see the main roof support falling over your head, that you will never survive. There are many cases where six to twelve inches of rock have killed many fine coal miners, yet there were four feet of stone lying on my back.

The second thought I had was I was going to heaven. The peace I experienced while falling to the earth was overwhelming and indescribable. Yet when I opened my eyes, there was total darkness, and my next thoughts were, *I must still be alive on earth because this sure isn't heaven!*. It was then I began praying, "Psalm 91, Lord! Psalm 91!" There was no possible way any man could have breathed under such a pile of rock, yet an angel of God had to be there keeping the rock pressure off me enough to breathe. It was difficult, but I could breathe. The Psalm 91 scripture I was saying between breaths was one of my mother's and grandmother's favorites. As I was fighting for my life under the stone, the crew of miners were risking their own lives, trying to uncover me by dragging layers of broken stone off of me. They later revealed to me they had little hope that I had survived the roof fall. The book cover shows me about to be loaded into the ambulance.

After my recovery, Tom Lindsay told me, "JT, we all knew you were a goner when we could only see your boots sticking out of all of that rock. When we took that last rock off of you, I swear to god that you were flat as a f—kin pancake." Indeed, there was a miracle in the mountains that day as many coal miners and mine inspectors realized that supernatural intervention had to have occurred for anyone to survive such a disaster. I was quick to tell all that it was God who took care of me that day. My testimony went even further as I told many that regardless of my fate that day, God would have taken care of me either way, whether I had lived or died.

My older brother, Mark Thomas, was a minister and had died of cancer earlier that year. My accident was another trying time for the Thomas family as internal bleeding was a concern for the medical staff as they tended to my wounds.

Mark was ill most of his life, yet despite over forty surgeries, four kidney transplants, and a drug overdose, he was an inspiration to all who knew him. His life was a storm within itself, yet he loved life and dedicated his life to ministry after he miraculously survived a drug overdose. He cherished each day as if it were his last. While lying in the hospital bed in Buckhannon, West Virginia, I recalled some of the last words my brother spoke to me. "I've faced death many times in life, bro Jamie, and this one (cancer) doesn't scare me either. I have no fear of death." I was with my brother the next week when at the age of forty years old, Mark went on to his reward.

However, it wasn't until three months later on August 12th that I truly understood what he was saying. For surely, death was now at my door in that dark coal mine, yet I had no fear, only peace and blessed assurance, when the mountain collapsed. It was not my time to go as my work here on earth was not finished. That was in 1996, and it wasn't until twenty five years later that these twenty four journeys would be remembered and printed in this book. As I began assembling this book, many storms arose, as my loving father passed away at the age of ninety two. He was a proud navy man and WWII veteran who loved God and his country. He and his father were coal miners as well. Our newly built home also had a waterline break, and our first floor became a pond. Then the love of my life of over thirty-six years had a heart attack. Thankfully, the Lord brought her safely through. Finally, came the last major storm when much of the transcript of this book was mysteriously lost on my computer. I took my computer to a professional, and he discovered the file had been somehow deleted. Perhaps, the greatest hurdle was to fight off the darts of Satan that constantly battled me in writing this book. Despite all of these sudden storms, I struggled through to bring you these twenty-four journeys that God will take you in 2022. I assure you that it is not for my benefit that God called me to his ministry and to write this book, but for yours. While many dreams, stories, and experiences found in the Bible may seem to about one individual, the message is to all of us. You will see that while each of the stories of the Holy Scriptures have a particular message, they all move to one message: continue reading, and you will get *the* message. I personally take no credit for the wisdom and knowledge God has given me as it is a gift for me only to share with others. I cannot thank him enough for the privilege and honor to be one of his chosen servants.

I would like to honor God for saving my life in that dark coal mine back in 1996 and to him, my loving mother, Mabel Thomas, and to my brother, Mark, I dedicate this book. Now we will begin our journey into times and places that God will take you in 2022.

> He that dwelleth in the secret place of the most High shall abide under the shadow of the Almighty.
> I will say of the Lord, His is my refuge and my fortress: my God; in him will I trust.
> Surely he shall deliver thee from the snare of the fowler, and from the noisome pestilence.
> He shall cover the with his feathers, and under his wings shalt thou trust: his truth shall be thy shield and buckler.
> Thou shalt not be afraid for the terror by night; nor for the arrow that flieth by day;
> Nor for the pestilence that walketh in darkness; nor for the destruction that wasteth at noonday.
> A thousand shall fall at thy side, and ten thousand at thy right hand; but it shall not come nigh thee.
> Only with thine eyes shalt thou behold and see the reward of the wicked.
> Because thou hast made the Lord, which is my refuge, even the most High, thy habitation;
> There shall no evil befall thee, neither shall any plague come nigh thy dwelling.
> For he shall give his angels charge over thee, to keep thee in all thy ways.
> They shall bear thee up in their hands, lest thou dash thy foot against a stone.
> Thou shalt tread upon the lion and adder: the young lion and the dragon shalt thou trample under feet.

Because he hath set his love upon me, therefore will I deliver him: I will set him on high, because he hath known my name.

He shall call upon me, and I will answer him: I will be with him in trouble: I will deliver him, and honour him.

With long life will I satisfy him, and shew him my salvation. (Psalm 91)

# INTRODUCTION

To prepare for the reading of this book, we will begin with a message from Thomas Mountain. A brother in Christ recently called me for a spiritual matter, and he told me, "God said to call Jamie. 'Jamie is my child.'"

Not only am I his child, but I am a called child of the God of Abraham, Isaac, and Jacob. Some authors are called by Grandma or Grandpa, some by their past, and some just to make a few dollars. I have been called by God himself to write this book on your behalf, and it is not of my own undertaking. All profits made from this book will be used to spread the Gospel throughout the world.

The Called. The Chosen. The Faithful. I have been called by the Creator of the universe not just to salvation but to declare the truths of God to all of mankind. First and foremost, you need to know this before you read on. Why he chose me, a simple man from the coal mining hills of West Virginia, I'll never know. Yet, I greatly appreciate his calling as it has encouraged and strengthened me as He led me in this writing. It has been written for both those within God's family and those seeking to join his family as well. While I have served God in other ministries, this book is one of the main reasons he has called me to his ministry. He has been by my side through the thick and thin in these sixty years here on earth. What a friend he has been. It is of my utmost desire to be a faithful child and a faithful servant to such an awesome and wonderful God.

I assure you that God never changes as he still calls imperfect people to serve him and proclaim his message. The Bible is full of servants who were far from perfect, and I would top the list if one were made. I do not claim to be a prophet but simply one to stoke the fire that they had for revealing the mind of God. This is a tremendous responsibility one undertakes to do just that. I, in no way, would ever want to lead one of his flock astray. It is with great boldness and strength given to me from God to get this book completed. Many may find this book difficult to read and accept, yet it is my prayer that it contributes to one's salvation.

I am a sinner yet saved by the grace of God. Just as God gave Gideon a sign for his calling in the book of Judges, so he did with me in the beautiful hills of Pendleton County, West Virginia.

I will share my experience of his wonderful calling later in this book. Don't bother burying me with some other servants that have been mocked and ridiculed throughout the ages. Many of them were so-called doomsday preachers, in which they thought the end of the age was drawing near. Some have been criticized, yet they were at least serving as a watchman for humanity. Those souls in eternity that turned due to their ministry, I assure you, are not mocking them now. This book references those in eternity numerous times and for good reason.

In heaven, it's all about others and the *focus* is on the stage here on earth. On earth, it's all about *self-interest, and the focus is most certainly not on heaven.* Drastic events are on the horizon here on planet earth and we should all be focusing on God. We must be informed and ready as both powers of God and of evil are moving in heaven and earth. We need to be moved by the power of God. Many servants of the past have come and gone while their messages were, at times, controversial. Many of them were merely sounding the alarm to awaken and move mankind closer to God as the last days are approaching.

Many of those servants made mistakes, yet God's Word never returns void (Isaiah 55:11). It is powerful regardless of who speaks it. I won't criticize any servant living or deceased, as many have done, but would commend any effort to get souls prepared to meet our Creator. Perhaps the greatest message given by all those in the past and present is that of anticipation.

## WHAT GOD WANTS YOU TO KNOW IN 2022

This mindset of anticipation follows us into eternity. It is directly related to our faith as well as our reward. It is impossible to please God and to be in his family without faith. It is also impossible to have faith without anticipation. As we study the scriptures in our infancy, we discover more and more about God, and that fuels our mind, our soul, and our spirit. It ignites a fire within us. A fire that enlightens the world. (Matthew 5:14) A fire fueled by the very presence of God. It is then, and only then, that we live a life of expectancy, a life of anticipation. We know we are just here for a moment, then with great expectancy and with great faith, we are assured we will be with him forever.

While on earth, our prayer is for "thy kingdom come." We expect him to come. We anxiously await his appearing while on earth. The early church did exactly this, and we continue, to this day, to live a life of anticipating his imminent return. It is again a result of our faith in him. The scriptures are clear that we must look for his return. (Luke 21:36) Yet, many who are called of God have been ridiculed for their doomsday message. Those who are critical of these servants could very well have a low or no degree of anticipation for the return of Christ. Having faith in God is placing our trust and assurance in Him and His Holy Word. Those who left this world of the early church (two thousand years ago) left this world expecting the Son of God to return at any moment. Now we too are doing the same, though the world stage is now set for his imminent return. So those presently in heaven as well as those about to arrive there have one thing in common—their faith and trust in God would ultimately deliver them there. God's Word assures us deliverance to heaven when our body ceases to live or when the rapture occurs. Christ will return to receive those who anticipate his return and love his appearing.

God's message of salvation and judgment proclaimed by his servants have been ridiculed in the past, yet the servant's message converted many souls. Their message brought many souls to the valley of decision. Those in the pit of darkness would tell you that while living on earth, they had moments when the call and light of God shone upon them. They could, in fact, define the moments that they felt called and saw the light of truth for a period of time. Yet, the glimpse of light given by God slowly vanished as their eyes turned away from the light and back to their worldly idols.

This book hopefully will provide another glimmer of hope and light to some as God leads me in writing this book. Sometimes, it takes drastic measures on earth for man to come to this valley. *What God Wants You to Know in 2022* is a book that hopefully will bring you to this valley. Where you go from there is on your dime, but remember, you can only spend it once.

While I have served God in many ways after my calling, I've always been led to write a book. It wasn't a matter of when I chose to write it but when God wanted it to arrive in your hands. The time he chose is now as the world is in great need of the message it contains.

The Bible has been the mainstay of my reading material for my entire lifetime of sixty years. There is no better reading material that is so rich in true substance as it reveals the mind of God. There is nothing more valuable on earth than the Word of God. Many feel that we are in the last days, and the time of tribulation (Daniel and Revelation) is about to begin. They could be right as we observe the world today. We have witnessed a dry barren land turn into a prosperous thriving country as prophecies of Israel's return began to be fulfilled in 1948. We also are witnessing a "falling away" as church attendance throughout Europe and the rest of the world is in rapid decline. The moral decline of the world has taken it's toll and it is only getting worse. We are also witnessing more war and rumors of war as we see in Europe and the Middle East. The COVID pandemic also has shook the world and the possibility of another deadlier strain could add more pestilence throughout the world. Knowledge and technology is increasing exponentially as prophesied in the Book of Daniel.

The division in America and throughout the world has gone to a new level, which creates concern when we look into the precious eyes of our children and grandchildren. Our enemy is working overtime to destroy the country that was fought for and founded by God-fearing people. What America needs is not more democrats or more republicans in Washington. What America needs is more elected officials that fear and trust in the God of Abraham, Isaac, and Jacob. Be careful not to focus on Washington in these days of uncertainty, but to meditate and focus on the Prince of Peace and the Almighty God. These events we are witnessing are of no surprise to them. Those, in office, regardless of one's party affiliation, must carefully consider each and every time they make a decision for the American people. It is my prayer that any decision and vote made gives honor and glory to God. He led us to this "promised land," and we must always remember that. On another positive note, we might consider that the virus has caused people to slow down and reflect on their lives and their overall position in life. The spirit of lawlessness is growing in America and abroad, and the only thing standing in its way are those who have the spirit of law, God's law, in their hearts and souls.

> **Blessed is the man that walketh not in the counsel of the ungodly, nor standeth in the way of sinners, nor sitteth in the seat of the scornful. But his delight is in the law of the Lord: and in his law doth he meditate day and night.** (Psalm 1:1–2)

Those who cannot see this spiritual uprising of evil must not only finish this book but they must decide, when in the valley of decision, which side you are on (Luke11:23). You are either on the Lord's side you're on Satan's side. There is no neutrality. To not be for him is to be against him, as many have turned their minds away from the truth of God.

> **For the time will come when they will not endure sound doctrine, but after their own lusts shall they heap to themselves teachers, having itching ears. And they shall turn away their ears from the truth, and shall be turned unto fables.** (2 Timothy 4:3–4)

With all the turmoil and uncertainty dominating the news today, one has to imagine, just what is next? Please don't journey down the road of despair as it is a tool of the enemy, Satan, to discourage and confuse the human race. Just because he has lost the hope of a bright future doesn't mean you have to. This book will reveal to all that there is joy that cometh in the morning, if you will only open your eyes to it. It is a gift and a calling to everyone. God will walk with you in the early morning. He is seeking fellowship with you as he dresses the beautiful sky each and every morning.

**"That they may know from the rising of the sun, and from the west, that there is none beside me. I am the Lord, and there is none else."** (Isaiah 45:6)

I have been blessed in so many ways in this short lifetime, and nothing thrills me more than to share the source of these blessings to all who seek him.

Seek God while he may be found.

Seek God while you have the ability to respond to his calling.

While I may not be highly educated, I am yet wonderfully blessed. I was raised in the coal mining hills of West Virginia by the best parents and with the best siblings one could ask for. Being a son of a coal miner, we were not rich in material things but rich in family values. Our parents taught us to honor God and enjoy the outdoors that he created. Praise and thanksgiving go to the Father for such a wonderful family. I pray his blessings and guidance upon you as you read on.

While I have experienced many battles in writing his book, I have realized it has been in God's timing that it has finally been completed.

God definitely works in mysterious ways. I consider myself a simple man conveying a simple message to a complex and diverse world that is in desperate need of it. It is a world growing in division and chaos. God's message has always been simple, yet man misconstrues it as Satan deceives the heart and mind of those without the

# WHAT GOD WANTS YOU TO KNOW IN 2022

Spirit of God (1 Corinthians 2:14). Satan is the god of deception as we clearly see how he is slowly and meticulously deceiving humanity in the world today. It will only get worse as God will eventually allow Satan to have more power as the end of the age nears. It is only a part of his judgment upon those who have rejected his love and salvation (Jeremiah 30:23–24). While Satan is currently having his way in chaos and confusion, God is ultimately in control and will fully restore order and peace upon the earth. His desire is that you might join him in eternity. Before this happens, judgment and cleansing must be completed by God. We could very well be witnessing the beginning of labor pains Jesus spoke of in Matthew 24:8.

The Bible is full of amazing stories, and we all enjoy good stories. So what would the story be if we were to go back in time to to the twenty-second verse of each book of twenty chapters? We will use this verse (and the verse before it) to take us back in time to that very place. So each journey will come from chapter 20 and will place you in the twenty-first and twenty-second verses. Therefore, now you will know what God wants you to know in 2022! These twenty-four journeys are intriguing and truly amazing as each one builds upon the other and ultimately grows into one huge message. The message of this book could not have been published at a better time. I hope you get God's message as we journey on. We must first begin with a personal question and self-evaluation.

Where are you really in position with God? Do you really have internal peace, a true feeling of purpose and a deep assurance of hope and security? Your answer may not be good as many souls are sinking in deceit and being fooled by the *greatest tragedy* facing all of mankind—placing *value* on things that have absolutely *no value*.

One may also address this tragedy of spending their entire lifetime *incorrectly* identifying *true substance and true reward*. Material things and stuff on earth are contributing to the demise of many as time pursuing the valueless has dulled the spiritual senses of many. This is nothing new for humanity. Wanting, stealing, coveting all this stuff and its pleasures has taken the world by storm. The idols may be dressed differently, but they still have the same disastrous result of serving self rather than serving God. There are few who are truly willing to be rid of these idols and to serve and love the Creator who made them. Be included in the few that truly loves God. Those who do love Him seek fellowship with Him and strives to be obedient to His will. If you've never pursued Him, you never knew Him.

Just how do you plan to spend eternity? We all have things to look forward to as we get older in life; however, when we are nearing the end of our life, then what next? Many lives are ended suddenly and unexpectedly and there is no time left to reconcile with God. There is absolutely no value in material things we now have when we enter the presence of God.

In Matthew 6:19–21, Jesus tells us that where your treasure is, there is where your heart is also. He goes on to say to put your treasures in things that moth and rust don't corrupt and thieves do not steal from you. Consider this truth and invest in true treasures that last forever.

Speaking of value, another huge mistake made by man is neglecting the value God has placed upon man. Yes, you. Have you ever considered the vastness of the universe and the uniqueness of Earth? We have certainly spent billions of dollars observing the beauty of it and have found no other planet like our own. The earth in her beauty is a marvel to behold, considering the vastness of the universe. It was perfectly made to support life for man and animals. You can also have this beautiful planet.

**Blessed are the meek; for they shall inherit the earth.** (Matthew 5:5)

Now that I have your attention, please consider this, God not only made this place for you, but he desires fellowship with you. You don't desire to go out and play football or basketball with a monkey. You don't want to go on vacation with a cow. You don't want to eat dinner with a bunch of hyenas. You desire to do all these things with souls like yours. No other creature on earth has a soul like that of man. Just as you want to enjoy fellowship with other human beings, so God, likewise, yearns to be with you and his family upon this earth. He values you so much that he uniquely made a habitation for you that he will eventually renew. The earth has to be purified and made holy for our Father to return and dwell among us for eternity. You must carefully understand that you will always be you. God respects your interests and your inner self as this defines your soul and spirit. Our new body, which is one of our rewards, will house our true self for eternity. We, too, must be purified. He never changes who you are but changes what you are after you become truly saved. You, being committed to his Son, have changed your position with God from being cursed to being blessed and spiritually "born again." Never forget that you will always be yourself whether you enjoy the new heavens and the new earth, or you are eternally suffering behind the gates of hell. Therefore, seek God now while he may be found. You were made in his image and his likeness.

He wants to be your provider, your friend, and your Father. He wants to restore all things including the house (our old body) we live in. The heavens, the earth, and those in the family of God all get renewed, and all pain, all suffering and all sin will be gone forever. Even the curse of the earth will soon be removed—this is the hope the family of God has.

Sin created by man separated us from this loving God in the Garden of Eden. God provided the means for us to overcome this sin that forbids us to enter this renewed earth. The means that He gave us to overcome was most precious and dear to him (his Son) to sacrificially give his life so we can be reunited with him, forever. His Son was perfect. His Son was not just another sacrifice, it was the *atonement for all of our sins*. Just as one man condemned the entire human race (Adam), the Son of God provided the atonement once for all those who place their faith and trust in him and his finished work.

Look up at the stars. Enjoy the warmth of the sun. Listen to the waves of the ocean soothing the mind. Sit by the crystal-clear streams flowing in the mountains. Look at the beautiful mountains as they turn color in the spring and fall in all their beauty. All the gold in the world cannot match the beauty of the golden aspen trees of Colorado during the autumn time of the year. All of this was made for you, and the best is yet to come. I cannot wait to see this earth after it is renewed. It is hard to conceive how it can be more beautiful than it currently is, but it will be because God will be with us. What beauty it will be to behold. (Psalm 27:4)

Never forget the true *value* God has placed on *you*.

Now consider the *value* that *you* have truly placed on him.

Eternity is real, and the souls there number into the billions. It may be worthwhile to consider what they have to say about true substance and real value. There is perhaps no better source other than God and his Word concerning true substance.

Let's ponder for just a moment and consider just what do all those in eternity have now? What would they say to you about value now? Eternity is the last thing many on earth think of on earth, yet its reality is there, especially to those who are already there. We must all, for a moment, consider what *they* have to say about *true substance*. While their message to us cannot be heard, their message can be revealed to us by considering their destination. Their destination (the result of their life) would be their greatest message to you and me. I assure you that your loved ones that have passed on have a message they would love to get to you as they are experiencing their eternal home. Jesus spoke of the rich man who sent himself to hell, and we get just a glimpse of the suffering that exists there. The rich man pleaded for even a drop of water to quench his thirst. It is now two thousand years later, and he has yet to get that drop of water. His desire will never be met. His pain, torment, and regret are all that exists for this man. He also pleaded for a way to warn his five brothers (Luke 16:26) of this pit of darkness and torment. While this warning never made it to his brothers, it did make it to those readers of the Bible and this book. Hell is real, my friend. Don't send yourself there. You are either a participant of a second birth (spirituality born into the family of God), or you are a participant in the second death. Those refusing to be in Christ will be sentenced to an eternal destiny in hell. This sentence is made to all the unsaved in the great white throne judgment.

The sense of warning you now feel isn't coming from Satan, nor the rich man, but the warning is coming from the Holy Spirit of God.

Again, every former millionaire in hell would give everything they had on earth to be sitting in your place right now. Because right now, you have the ability to be saved from the fate they are now suffering in. That is forever.

*Most* of humanity will never enter heaven and the new earth, but have chosen the pit of darkness under the earth for their eternal dwelling. Never forget it was by their choice they are there. Those facing God in judgment must answer for themselves, and no other influence, no person and no reason will justify entry into the glorious kingdom of God. Those in the pit have no leverage whatsoever to change the mind of God nor their eternal home of suffering. Those in the pit would want you to know the *value* you possess *of having the ability* to choose and grasp the hand of God.

By their rejecting the helping hand of God, they have rejected his wisdom, his will, his sovereignty, his redemption, his reward, and most of all, his *fellowship forever.* Their life on earth entailed placing value on everything but the precious gift offered to them of grasping the love and hand of God. They could all blame Satan, yet he just planted the seeds of rebellion. Pure selfishness of the heart and soul turned them from the light of God to the eternal pit of darkness.

This refusal has blotted their name out of the Book of Life, the book which takes those in the family of God to heaven and to our new earth. God yearns to be with us on this planet. However, most of those before us choose not to take his hand. Regretfully, this decision takes them to a pathway of eternal separation from the God of light and the God of love. Please remember, all those in this eternal place of darkness have rejected the hand of God, which forfeited their entry into the new heavens and the new earth.

> **I am come a light into the world, that whosoever believeth on me would not abide in darkness. And if any man hear my words, and believe not, I judge him not: for I came not to judge the world, but to save the world. He that rejecteth me, and receiveth not my words, hath one that judgeth him, the word that I have spoken, the same shall judge him in the last day.** (John 12:46–48)

The humility and meekness of God is unsurpassed. He merely says, "Call upon the name of the Lord and thou shalt be saved." He will hear your prayer, and his helping hand will cling to yours and will never let go. To believe in him is to *be in him*, not just some lip service and a dollar in the offering plate at Christmas. Jesus first came to save the world, and you are in luck as you are still living in the window of opportunity to accept him as Lord and Savior. But you must read the last part of the scripture in John 12 as it states that Christ will be the judge in the last day. You see, judgment is coming, whether you are ready or not.

**For God so loved the world that he gave his only begotten Son, that whosoever believeth in him should not perish, but have everlasting life**. (John 3:16)

Again, the humility and meekness of God is just short of amazing as he puts up with us stiff-necked rebellious bunch of humans. I am not just speaking of Israel, as we all fit into this category. In all of his power, he could merely make us all serve him, and we could well be on our way. Or better yet, he could destroy us with his breath and create another people who would be more obedient and appreciative toward him. Yet he doesn't, and he simply wants you to choose to be with him. The degree of love and patience our Father has for each of us can never be described but can most certainly be felt and observed by those who seek and follow him.

The journeys in this book will reveal stories of individuals, kings, priests, and many others who have taken his hand as well as those who refused his hand. Much is to be learned from the past, and these journeys certainly have profound, yet simple, messages. I assure you, there are many in eternity who would give anything to be in your shoes right now. You are now in the driver's seat, but remember, only for a *moment*. You may choose to commit to God, or perhaps you may choose to follow him more closely. Choose you this day who you will serve as tomorrow may never come. Don't be deceived in thinking your life has been a waste with no chance of regaining any purpose. Satan will beat you down with discouragement, but remember God's strength is far greater. There is a given power of hope and purpose available for the asking by our Creator, regardless of your age. It's never to late to turn to God, as a little reward in heaven is far better than suffering eternally in hell.

While many in the pit of darkness were the wealthiest on earth, the pain and regret will be unbearable as they now find themselves totally helpless. While upon earth, these people had anything they wanted with the snap of their fingers. Unfortunately, they now have no power nor any right to change their position or their destination. They have all of eternity to regret a short lifetime chasing things and seeking things that now have absolutely *no value*. They pursued worldly power and pleasure and neglected the power of the blood of Christ which could have delivered them.

Many of you reading this book are headed for the same destiny. Listen closely and you might hear the pain and anguish from those in the pit. I once heard that one of the deepest holes drilled on earth (in Russia) producing a chilling result—some could hear, at times, the screams of those in the pit. Now I am not certain of the truth in this, but it remains a possibility. There is no question, however, that the pit of darkness exists, and only God knows its location.

All of those in the pit are guilty of refusing the love and the hand of God. The realization that those they considered their enemies (true believers) while living on earth were actually their *true friends*. The true believers were prayerfully trying to pull the lost out of the fire they are now in. Be careful not to condemn or ridicule those in your life who are doing just that. There will be no party in hell. Their destiny was unfortunately developed by simply placing more value on self-interest than trying to seek and serve God and to help others. Those old buddies(friends) surrounding them on earth merely contributed to their fiery destination.

Old friendships perish in hell. Those old relationships quickly and perpetually turn into a shouting match in the darkness. The finger-pointing once used on earth against God's children is redirected to those "old friends" who contributed to their horrible destination.

I cannot understand why so many good people let trivial things become a means to separate them from the God who made them.

We are to enjoy his creation and worship him; however, most worship his creation and neglect and forget the Creator. So, choosing things of no eternal value is the norm for most of humanity as the Word of God clearly states that many are called, yet few are chosen. Regardless of what you read and hear, his hand is extended *to all*. But he only chooses those who reach for his hand. Rejecting his hand causes you to choose eternal darkness as your reward when life on earth has ended. Those in the pit wanted nothing of this "God stuff" on earth, and that is just what they will get forever. There is no escape and no appeals for the massive multitudes yearning for a pardon.

After the earth was created, there was little need for volcanoes, but the tragedy man created in the Garden of Eden may have changed the need for volcanoes. Because of the sinful actions of Adam and Eve, billions of souls will be delivered to spend eternity under the earth in the pits of hell forever. As we see the hot lava pouring out of the earth, during a volcanic eruption, we may be witnessing the expansion of hell, making more room for those who have rejected God. Hell is enlarged by the multitudes that merely reject his grace and plan of redemption (Isaiah 5:14). Take a moment and search "British scientist finds hell on earth." This image may quite well be hell venting herself. Also, search "Scientist in Siberia digs into hell" as it also supports the truth of the existence of hell. Finally, one more interesting article to research is the recent discovery of another layer of the earth's crust by our scientists.

The headlines in heaven's newspapers are far from ours here on planet Earth. Remember Satan is the prince of the air in the world and is at work spreading deception and propaganda throughout the world. Anything not supported by God's Word is a lie, and Satan is the father of lies. As mankind focuses on his worldly desires, the heavenly realm focuses on family and others. It's headlines honor the kingdom of God and rejoice when the kingdom is enlarged by one soul grasping the hand of God. One must carefully consider their current identity and position in heaven. Now when you see images from the Hawaiian Island eruptions and those eruptions of the past, just remember, you could very well be witnessing the pits of hell enlarging herself.

Your life right now is making preparations somewhere. Preparations for a chair and a dinner plate is being made in heaven (Revelation 19), or you're about to make the earth erupt again to make a place for you in the underworld of the dead (Isaiah 14). This chapter in Isaiah also confirms the final destiny of Satan himself as those in hell observe the guy who guided them there. There is no more mocking those "hell-bent Christians," but the deceiver himself is getting mocked now by all of the deceived. Don't be a part of this event as it will happen someday. You are now no longer deceived as you have heard the truth and know the truth. The truth of Christ will set you free.

Speaking of heaven, just what would all of those in heaven say to us on earth? The message of those in heaven is the same message those in hell would be quick to tell us, "*Draw nigh to God*", and "*Take the hand of God while you still can!*" take the hand of God now where there's still time! Many are in eternity pleading to get this message to their loved ones and friends: "take his hand and follow Christ now. I assure you there are those in eternity who are pleading for their loved ones to commit and follow Jesus Christ.

Just as the volcanoes of the past may testify of the earth needing room for the rebellious and the selfish, the stars of heaven reveal the number of souls that chose the hand of God. Also take a stroll along the beautiful beaches of the earth and look down at the sands of the sea. Here is another example of those choosing the hand of God as he promised Abraham his descendants would both be as the stars of heaven and of the sands of the sea,

> **"That in blessing I will bless thee, and in multiplying I will multiply thy seed as the stars of the heaven, and as the sand which is upon the sea shore; and thy seed shall possess the gate of his enemies"** (Genesis 22:17).

Wow. The old faithful saints of old and those accepting the atonement of Christ's blood are shining bright! Walk the beautiful beaches and stare at the beautiful stars, and even better, make your reservation in the sky. This is a much more pleasant sight to be a part of than falling into a pit made by a violent volcano. Now is the time to reflect upon your life and where you are going for eternity.

As the major concern here is not what you have *done* nor what *you plan* to do, the major concern is what are *you doing now*?

**I am crucified with Christ: nevertheless I live, yet not I, but Christ liveth in me: and the life I now live in the flesh I live by the faith of the Son of God who loved me, and gave himself for me.** (Galatians 2:20)

We should give special attention to some of the last words and messages the Son of God gave us in the book of Revelation. Perhaps some of his last words should be the first words we consider in our daily lives. We see Christ addressing the churches in his initial address to the apostle John. He addresses what they were doing then as we should address what we are doing now (as a follower and as a church). These shortfalls and serious faults were problems in the early church and the same problems exist in our churches today. The status of the church individually and collectively is described in Revelation 2–3. Christ addresses the shortfalls and major problems that must be overcome by his followers. We must acknowledge both our position in Christ as well as our practice (our daily lifestyle) in Christ as we carefully identify "overcoming" in the scriptures. The apostle John specifically tells us in John 5:5 that those who have truly confessed Jesus to be the Son of God (and believed in their heart) gives us the *position* of overcoming the debt of sin we owe as well as the curse we are under to be in the family of God. Yet, we see John also sees by the warnings Jesus gave him in writing the book of Revelation, that believers (the church) are subject to rewards as well as consequences for neglecting and dishonoring Christ. Being truly saved is like being a cancer patient who is given a lifesaving prescription for their disease. Yet, the bottle clearly states the drug has to be taken daily. Too often, we forget to "take our medicine" daily as we neglect Christ in our prayer life and studying his Word.

John tells us in 3:16 that to "believe *in Him*" and being "in him" is a daily effort to be more like him and to desire to be with him. Consider your day. Where did you spend your time? How much of it did you consider, honor, seek, thank, and praise the *ONE* who gave you the power and the position to "overcome"? Paul said "I die daily" in explaining that our focus must be on Christ as we face our struggles each and every day.

Beware of Satan and his deceitful ways to discourage those in the family of God.

Satan is always distracting the minds of those seeking a closer relationship with God. You *are* either *in* the battle as a believer, or *you are* the battle as a follower of Satan. Satan is a master of deceit and distractions when it comes to serving and honoring God. We must be overcomers as the Son of God enables us to become. Jesus also mentions the overcomers toward the end of the book,

**"He that overcometh shall inherit all things; and I will be his God and he shall be my son"** (Revelation 21:7).

Not many have the luxury of knowing just when their final breath on earth will come. Regardless of one's past and some's current ill-fated future, any person breathing right now *has the ability* to change the course of their current life as well as the jewel of a peaceful and safe eternity. Whether your intent is to take the hand of God or to do more for his kingdom, neither intent, in itself, will give you a "hill of beans." The Bible is filled with great stories of action, and we need to act on what is deep within our hearts. It has been quoted many times that the road to hell is paved with good intentions. It is well said. Faith without works is dead, just as James told us (James 2:26).

If you truly want peace, purpose, substance, equity, and security in your life, open your mind, heart, and spirit and read on because the narrow gate is open that leads us to the pathway of righteousness and true wisdom. Wisdom is calling you. Wisdom will respond if you inquire. Wisdom will deliver you if you turn from self to servant. A window is open for many at this moment in time. The narrow path is now in full view. Opportunity of indescribable rewards and true substance is available to those who seek it. While this gift was extremely costly in heaven, it is free to all who are living upon this earth. It is only by the grace and mercy of God that we can obtain it.

While wisdom is a gift from God, it must be *recognized*, then *desired*, and ultimately *pursued* by those who recognize it. Therefore, it must be actually heard, then *sought out*, and then *chased*. Notice *action* is required here. For some, it is a sprint. For some, it is a marathon. For some, it is a brisk walk. For some, it is a mere crawl, but for all the above, it is an *action* of turning away from self and trusting in the God of truth. It's where *faith* in true substance comes into play. While those in the pit only have regret and judgment of their life awaiting them, those in heaven have already received much of their reward by having been delivered and secured to the eternal presence of God. Their deeds done while on earth have their own reward, which will be tried with fire.

The sprinters will receive rewards comparable to gold, and the marathon runners will have rewards comparable to silver. Those walking and crawling will have a reward of simply being accepted into the glorious kingdom as their deeds are burned up as hay and stubble. They did little, but they did something. So I assure you, those in eternity could give us a *pure* definition of *true substance*. All of us on earth have no right to judge nor to speak ill of one another nor to attempt to determine one's status with God.

Only God sees the heart and *intentions* of man. We have absolutely no right nor the ability to judge one's status with the Almighty God. We are also not qualified to determine one's rewards, whether they be good or bad. God-fearing people are the minority now on earth, and most folks don't love God nor truly serve him. While that fact is supported by God's Word, we have no right nor the ability to define and judge those souls. Leave those things up to our Heavenly Father and pray for those in your circle. Pray for those you are on stage with. I assure you, there are those in your pathway who God has led you to and there are also those sent into your life for a purpose as well.

False religions are based on traditions and emotional feelings that the enemy uses to give a false sense of peace that never lasts. False religion strives for man to save himself and that also fails. We must not be fooled with these false religions that appear to be genuine but are counterfeits. Despite all the feelings and emotional experiences that are encountered in false religions, they can never deliver us from the deep guilt we all have caused by our sinful and rebellious nature toward God. No works in their greatest effort can deliver us out of this darkness—absolutely none.

There exists a vacuum within every soul to seek our true Creator. That is because we are a part of him as we were made in his own likeness. Our soul and spirit contains an emptiness that can be filled by our Creator. It is unfortunate that most of humanity attempts to fill that vacuum with everything but the *true faith* in God which ultimately delivers true peace. Any religion that does not identify Jesus as the Son of God, his finished work on the cross, and his resurrection is not of God. There are those who say there are many ways to heaven, but actually, there is only one way, and that is through faith in the Messiah. Jesus Christ was the anointed one and while He didn't deliver the Jews from Roman rule, He did so much more by delivering both Jew and Gentile from the bondage of sin.

You never hear of true Christians wasting time and energy on searching for our origin or how old the earth is. We must have faith in the Word of God found in the Holy Bible. While many try to find fault in the Bible and it's origin, it has harmony and unity to those whom the Spirit of God dwells. We are so privileged to have the living Word of God that beautifully spans from our beginning to eternity. We do know that mankind is approximately six thousand years old. We are so blessed with science and technology as they have enhanced our lives tremendously. However, science without our Creator being the source is in great error. Are you going to believe the highly debatable theory of carbon dating originating in the 1940s over the Word of God? Archeology is a wonderful tool and has been very useful in providing much of the Bible's history and validity.

Our enemy is the master of spreading confusion of our origin. Satan isn't that interested in getting you to cuss, or to steal as he strives relentlessly to keep you from believing the truth. Satan also despises the archeological finds that prove the stories and truths of the Bible. Have you heard our astronomers have now discovered huge amounts of gold in our universe? I can tell you it is a direct result of the street sweeping done in heaven! (Revelation 21:21)

The greatest finds of Archeology rest in the Holy Land. There is no other place on earth where so much excavation is being done. There is no other place on earth that proves our origin than the Holy Land. If a coin, a sword, a vessel, or even a city is discovered, there is always biblical evidence to support these artifacts. Historical records other than the Bible have also proven the accuracy of the Bible. The vast amounts of archeological discoveries have been biblically accurate, and more and more artifacts are unearthed each year.

Each of that bone, tool, vessel, or spear will tell a story that many times can be found in the Bible. The main problem is how man errs in attempting to date each object on faulty carbon dating. The powers of Satan have deceptively created misinformation in our origin, and faulty carbon dating is just one way he confuses mankind. No other source is available or accurate as the historical biblical record of the earth and mankind. Please take a moment and search "Erroneous carbon dating," and you will find many articles disproving the old radiocarbon dating method. These articles have basically said we must reevaluate the history books man has written. Yet what they are really saying is we need to quit wasting time and energy on this false data and rely on the biblical history recorded in minute details. Also now the proponents of evolution are realizing they might be a bit wrong as well. They need to alter their drawings to now match our true DNA. Don't you think that DNA would be similar in many aspects of life as a pattern of design comes into play? While there are similarities of DNA of man and other living beings, nothing has been *exactly* like ours but ours only.

One only has to study the magnificent design and function of our bodies to realize we are formed and designed intelligently by our Creator and did not evolve from a single cell in a murky swamp. It is so unfortunate that as many pursue and gain intellectually in life, they lose their spiritual common sense that God gave us all. Go to your quiet place, and ask God for wisdom and direction.

> **If any of you lack wisdom, let him ask of God, that giveth to all men liberally, and upbraideth not, and it shall be given him. But let him ask in faith, nothing wavering. For he that wavereth is like a wave of the sea driven with the wind and tossed.** (James 1: 5–6)

True wisdom only comes from God. Wisdom doesn't question how we got here or how old we are. Wisdom lies deep within one's heart and soul, confirming a sense we overlook as mere humans—the sense of our spirit uniting with the Spirit of God. It is an invitation to all as the Holy Spirit will knock on your heart's door. This marriage settles all of these profound questions, and *only* then is the landscape of true knowledge and wisdom truly and deeply revealed. Those without this Spirit, regardless of their education, are walking, talking, and teaching in darkness and deception. They have dangerously opened their house (mind, soul, and spirit) to invading and deceitful spirits which distort truth and basic reasoning. Many of our colleges and universities have professors who have abandoned the basic and logical reasoning that God has given to each of us. The truth of God is getting suppressed more and more by many of our highest educators. This suppression of truth has a devastating effect on the youth of our country. Parents are ultimately responsible for the spiritual leading and instruction in the family. If you neglect this responsibility, you and your children will suffer as a result. The acceptance and knowledge of God enters the vacuum of the soul and spirit, and the human mind is taken to a new level. When the heart is changed, so so is the mind. The mind is then enlightened as the eyes and ears are opened to spiritual wisdom and understanding.

As previously mentioned, the perfection of the human body could not have been by chance. Deep within every soul, we know this as there is nothing in this world nor in the universe that compares to our likeness and uniqueness. Our body and its function is a marvel to behold, and I am just an old former coal miner, but I realize it has to be by intelligent design. It is possible that some books written on our origin may have been authored by chimpanzees, but not this one. LOL.

The degree of wisdom and knowledge of every person is ultimately determined upon one's death. Just where do the angels take one when they passed from this short life to their permanent home? I assure you this happens as my mother, grandmother and great grandmother all saw angels just before they were taken to heaven. It has been said angels take God's children to heaven while demons take everyone else to hell. Know this; you are delivered to your eternal dwelling place by either angels or demons. Ultimately, it is your choice. Choose wisely.

One's destiny speaks volumes as to the true level of wisdom and knowledge they attained while living on earth. Life is a mere preparation for eternity. While life is tremendously short in relation to eternity, it provides a one-way ticket and passport to the gates of heaven. While the ticket has been purchased by the Son of God, it is redeemed the moment we die. Your angel not only has your back while on earth, but he also takes your back to your Creator! What a joy is to those who die in Christ. Those who refused the hand of God are ushered into the deep pits of the earth after they die. Our destiny instantly reveals a life spent chasing the wisdom of God or the wisdom of the world. We must turn to the wisdom of God to truly obtain peace, assurance, and security through *His* righteousness and truth.

As mentioned earlier, history contained in the Bible proves factual truth. Yes, the stones of the past discovered by archeologists reinforce all the truths of the Bible. This evidence of artifacts proves, over and over, the truth of the Holy Scriptures. Could you imagine the artifacts we would be unearthing if the theory of evolution was actually true? Remember the chart that shows us being a mere cell that evolved into other cells to become an ocean-like creature, then we crawled out of the ocean and grew into a half-fish, half-monkey, then a perfect human being? Wow. But there is just one problem to this great profound explanation to our origin. Where, in all the archeological findings, is there any real evidence of these creatures? Since we have "billions" of years there should be lots of evidence, right?

Exactly how many of these specimens have been unearthed? *None.* The phrase "missing link" was derived by those who were missing wisdom.

Creation itself reveals to each and every soul the one true living God. The God of Abraham, Isaac, and Jacob. It is truly impossible for us to see the beauty of the ocean and the mountains and rivers and the sunrise and the sunset and our beautiful animals and our beautiful children without seeing God. Anyone who claims otherwise is kidding themselves.

The beauty of creation is there for all of us, and it will do one of two things: it will all go to hell as a memory only, or it will get even more beautiful as the earth is renewed by God. Those in hell will have nothing but regret as they will never again see the beauty of God's creation. Those faithful to God will enjoy this renewed earth and its beauty forever. Your destiny right now is one of the two, and only you, my friend, can make that decision. Don't make the fatal and disastrous mistake of allowing emotions and feelings to drown out the calling of God to his saving grace and infinite wisdom. The sea of darkness will eventually take you deeper than you want to go. While in this sea of darkness, there is still hope, but those in the pit of eternal darkness (those who have died without Christ) have lost all hope, and there is no hope of a rescue. All there would love to see the sun rise, yet that day will never come in the pit. "They will never again witness the rising sun as they never witnessed for the risen Son while on earth."(Acts 1:8)

Emotional feelings produce no substance for the soul and spirit with no factual truth or power. It's like trying to run on junk food all the time and never getting good nutrition for the body. True faith in God is more than a feeling. True faith is believing that God's plan and promises to you are unshakable regardless of any kind of situation one may be experiencing. True faith keeps our eyes on our Creator and none other for our provisions and safety. In Him comes wisdom and understanding that assure us of His promises. True wisdom is calling every soul to true substance, true life, and true light.

Jesus Christ said, "I am the way, the truth and the life, and no man comes to the Father, but by me." The Bible is truth, and we can clearly see it's history and accuracy is unrivaled by any written or unwritten word. While other false religions have involved only parts of our history here on earth, God ensured through his scriptures our beginning as well as our end. Throughout history, other religions have tried to compare and even replace Christianity, but God has ensured us through His scriptures both our creation and our eternal destination. No other religion or so-called god comes close to attaining this crucial task. God carefully included everything we desire to know in his holy scriptures. We have to take it upon ourselves to study and meditate on the Word of God. As we search the scriptures, we discover precious gems of wisdom and understanding that no money can buy as we become spiritually satisfied and content in our discoveries. We should never be satisfied just to know of our Creator; we should yearn to know him more. There is a message for all of us when we study this great book of wisdom, the Holy Bible. The Word of God has been under attack since God first began communicating with us and before he authored the Bible. It all started when Satan asked Eve, "Did God really say?" (Genesis 3:3). While many wrote down our Holy Scriptures, it is ultimately God's message and his authorship. The Holy Spirit moved the prophets and called other servants to reveal God's message to all. Apostle Paul clearly stated that all scripture is inspired by God, to teach us the truth, to rebuke error, to correct our faults, and to give us instructions for living. These scriptures were given to qualify and equip us in serving and representing the Kingdom of God (2 Timothy 3:16).

If you have been overwhelmed or confused by the complexities of the Bible, hopefully this book and the twenty-four journeys will help you put things into a better perspective. This book was definitely not written as a replacement for the reading and searching of the scriptures, rather as a tool to bring the light to scriptures pertaining to the twenty-second verse following the twentieth chapter of the Bible, thus 20:22. Hopefully, these stories will encourage a deeper desire to study the entirety of the Bible.

These stories beautifully brings to us twenty-four places in time that takes us on twenty-four journeys, beginning around four thousand years ago, and leads us to our final destiny.

In a few cases, the twenty-second verse will go into the next chapter, but it is still the twenty first and twenty second verse from chapter 20. God has a message for each journey, so we must diligently search each scripture and the background associated with that verse. The journey this book takes you on will amaze you, strengthen you, and lead you to a closer walk with our Creator. This book is not for the one who knows it all, but for those wanting to truly know the *One* who does.

As addressed earlier, mankind has difficulty in assessing risks. There is an unfortunate and disastrous end to those who constantly refuse God's calling and his plan of reconciliation for his love—mankind. Make no mistake about it, *you* are his first love. He should be yours.

The Most High God and the Lord of hosts is literally reaching down from heaven to grasp our hand as humanity is in a spiritual sea of darkness. The reality is that you have either been delivered out of this darkness, or you are still treading in it hopelessly. Some are becoming weary and are beginning to sink into the eternal deep waters. Rest assured, God's hand is never so far away that it cannot rescue you.

You must grab his hand while you are able. There is little time left for many. Multitudes leave this *sea* of darkness of the world to enter *a deep pit* of darkness upon their deaths, and what a tragedy it is for them. Only God knows when your last day will come. His hand is always there, a nail-scarred hand that will safely pull *anyone willing* to believe to safety and eternal peace. There is an unknown danger ahead for many, and the contents of this book might be your final means for an eternal and desperate rescue. For many, this book may be the final wake-up call from God. Regardless of your status or position on earth, think of this life as a mere preparation for the real life, your eternal life, to come.

The hand of God will not be available for us forever, and we must take the *initiative* to grasp his hand while we have the *ability* to do so. He makes us aware of him and his calling, but he never invades our privacy as he has given us our own free will and choice.

Our *understanding, knowledge, and acceptance* of God is on *us*, not on him; this responsibility can be a beauty or a beast. However, God is constantly looking down from heaven to find those who truly seek him (2 Chronicles 6:30–31). Once you understand God and His message, you will immediately begin to seek more of Him. The risk factor is this: when God calls each person (seeks them), there has to be a response, whether it is positive or negative. The response to God's calling must be weighed by all, regardless of what one thinks. Again, *all* have been called to the knowledge of truth that only God can give, yet the question is, what is your response (Isaiah 45:21–22)?

> **Tell ye, and bring them near; yea, let them take counsel together: who hath declared this from ancient time? who hath told it from that time? have not I the LORD? and there is no God else beside me; a just God and a Saviour; there is none beside me. Look unto me, and be ye saved, all the ends of the earth: for I am God, and there is none else.**

Once the awareness and truth of God is made to each of us, it is ultimately *our* decision whether to accept and *follow* him or to *deny* him. Here is where most of humanity fail as they *refuse* this calling and his hand of rescue, and take the wide pathway. They unwisely choose the wide path of temporal things and pleasures over eternal wealth and security. It has been the demise of mankind from the beginning in the Garden of Eden and will continue until the end of the age. Eternal rewards that all the gold in the world cannot purchase are merely surrendered for selfish desires that are short-lived. Our enemy is not only the darkness of evil but also the carnal flesh that strives with our spirit and soul.

Always remember, it is one thing to know *about* God but another thing to *live* for him and to be dedicated to him. Many say they know God, and they pray to Him, but it is actually a god they have fabricated in their mind to fit their lifestyle. Beware of wolves in sheep's clothing and their teachings.

Remember, everyone has a god, but not everyone has God, the true and living God. Jesus himself said, "Not all those whom call me Lord, Lord shall enter into the Kingdom of Heaven." Those separated from God have no remorse for their sin. A thief has a mind of a thief. He is constantly thinking like a thief. He plans on stealing and does. He has no regret nor any remorse for taking what is not his. A coveter has a mind to covet. He constantly seeks things others have and is never content. As the envy grows, family, friends, and God are dishonored. This lifestyle of fabricating their own god ultimately pleases the flesh but ends in tragedy as Jesus tells all of humanity seven crucial words when we meet him. For the few, "Well done thy good and faithful servant," and for the many, "Depart from me ye worker of iniquity." Again, none of us can see the heart of another and, thus, should never judge them. None of us at our best behavior are exempt from sin as we all do. Search your own heart and deal with this reality that many are called but few are chosen. This book is intentionally calling on all of it's readers to evaluate their own position with God, and their true commitment to him as well. Too many folks are looking and pointing fingers at others only to their own demise. While we all stumble and fall as true believers, we should ultimately be pointing others to the saving grace and forgiveness of God. It is crucial, my friend, that you forgive one another just as Christ has forgiven you (Colossians 3:13).

A child of God, however, while he is tempted daily, still thinks as a child of God. Everyone struggles. The child of God struggles to serve him as life is certainly not a bed of roses for the follower of Christ. Each and every believer's level of maturity varies, yet he still strives to serve the Shepherd. It is not that he never sins, it is that he strives not to sin against God. While his life is a struggle, it ultimately is defined as a battle of the mind and flesh to be obedient to our heavenly Father. It's not easy, but within this struggle, we have inner peace and joy that is beyond description. These journeys lead us through a process of struggling, and it is God's intentions that we learn and grow from them. Grasping the hand of God gives us the power to overcome the forces of evil as we cannot do on our own strength. While it was other's day in the sun we journey to, today is our day in the sun, and we need to make the best of it while we can publicly proclaim the truth of the gospel. The Bible goes to great lengths to explain that mankind is approximately six thousand years old. Your entry is recorded there every single day. What have you done for the Lord lately?

It's that simple, my friend, being in the family of God means that you honor him and deeply appreciate his love and his provisions. You just simply *get it* when you get *him*. It doesn't mean to live a perfect life as critics of Christians are quick to point out. God never *seeks our perfection* as he knows none of us can ever acquire that pinnacle, even for a moment. Yet God seeks *our desire* to get to perfection. Christians desire to be *like him* and to be *with him*. While some rarely speak to God and some don't bother, there are a few who truly seek God. Be one of the few.

Christians have a deep respect for authority as we accept the authority and sovereignty of God. His instruction for us to honor our mother and father, as well as those in higher authority, ultimately lays the groundwork for honoring Him. Our struggle varies from one faithful believer to another, but it is real for all of us! As we approach the last days, the spirit of lawlessness begins to take hold more and more aggressively. This was foretold by the apostle Paul, and we see it clearly happening today (2 Thessalonians 2). Rebellion is sown early in the minds of our young children. It begins with rebelling against their parents, then their teachers, then their law enforcement officers, then ultimately against God the Father. The planter of rebellion is none other than Satan himself.

Don't get discouraged but rest in the promises of God. The gift of salvation to all of humanity can never be attained by our works but only of God the Father. It is a gift explained over and over in the Bible as a gift offered to only those living on earth. It is also only a gift that God can deliver. It is also a gift that *must* be *received* and *confessed*.

Again, you possess something that billions of souls in eternity would give *anything* for, and that is your *free will* to grasp the hand of God as *you still can*. It's better to grasp that hand with his smile than seeing that hand withdrawn to grasp his gavel. You are either eternally forgiven and accepted into the Kingdom of Heaven, or you are set for a sentencing date when you will be cast into hell. Every soul is a free moral agent, and it just happens to dwell in a body. Once the body deceases, the extended hand of God is withdrawn. Judgment is the event where each and every soul will give account for their life as the books are opened which reveal every minute detail of their life. Again their free will to reject or accept God on earth has sealed their fate and eternal destiny. Every soul on earth either chooses to honor God or dishonor him. Those souls in hell who dishonored God will be judged for all their sins but those who have honored God will have no record of sin, and will be judged according to what they accomplished with their faith in God. Again faith, without works is dead. After you are saved, faith moves you from an old self to a new creature in Christ. You are no longer under the curse of the Law but under the shed blood of the Son of God. This cleanses you from all unrighteousness. The level of faith varies with each soul and, again, this is not for us to judge. Yet it must be said that if there is no genuine change in one's heart, there is likely no change in one's actions. Carefully consider the fruit you have truly produced for the Kingdom of God. The world is full of chaos fueled by Satan, but we must continue the chaos Jesus started over two thousand years ago. While he presents himself as the Prince of peace to the few, most of the world is offended by him and his followers. To the wicked, he is creating chaos and disturbing the nest they have made in worldly pleasures and treasures. Following Christ was not popular then and isn't now.

> **Suppose ye that I am come to give peace on earth? I tell you Nay; but rather division. For from henceforth there shall be five in one house divided, three against two, and two against three.** (Luke 12:51–52)

There are no true atheists on earth and definitely none in hell. God never sends anyone to that outer darkness, yet vast multitudes there have one thing in common—they have all sent themselves into the pit of darkness (Romans 1:21–23). The hand of God does not randomly go throughout the sea of darkness and pick and choose whom He will save and whom He will not. He *only* pulls to safety those who take the *initiative* to grasp his hand. He will pull you out of the sea of darkness into his marvelous light.

**Draw nigh to God and he will draw nigh to you.** (James 4:8)

Many teachers err in promoting that God has predestined those whom he has chosen to become his sons and daughters. This has been perceived by some as you have no choice in your final destiny. Nothing is so far from the truth. This false belief has taken multitudes down the wrong path and has led many to believe there is no hope for them. Read John 3:16, and it will deny the belief that only some are called to be in the family of God. "Whosoever" includes you. If that were the case, why is there all the need for servants of God to spread the truth of the Gospel as described in Acts 1:8? Also, what would be the need to write this book? Again, remember this book at times visits the same message as there is little time left for many to turn to the narrow pathway leading to heaven. It is also my hope that it will strengthen the believer to a closer walk with God.

While it is true that God knew us before we were ever born, he does not predetermine our faith and commitment to him. While that invaluable decision *we alone* make is the driver that allows God to predestine our lives in this darkened world to proclaim the gospel of His Son in the sphere that we are living in. Now you know the plan God has for your role in life. Your life in God's family is there to shed the light of God to all those around you. God respects and wants to see mankind develop and mature in their own interests and he enjoys providing the means for this development in life. Remember we are made in his image and his likeness and he wants us to enjoy His creation.

While in college, there were those whom God wanted me to witness to. While in the US Air Force, there were those God wanted me to witness to during flight training in Enid, Oklahoma. While managing and working with the best coal miners in the world, there were those God wanted me to witness to. So it goes for all of us. At times, I was a poor witness, and other times, I was on fire for the gospel of the Lord Jesus Christ; yet nonetheless, it was where God wanted me at those times to tell of His truths. There is one particular friend who once told me that God sent me into the Air Force to lead him into a closer walk with God. This guy has been on fire for the Lord ever since and now is an inspiration to me. He now is on fire for Christ as he does mission work in Nicaragua. As I reflect upon when I was in officer school in Knoxville, Tennessee (Academy of Military Science), and also in flight training at Vance Air Force Base, I saw many God sent my way, and He did it for a reason. Many souls who had questions about God and eternity had been brought into my life. While I was attending Leivasy Grade School as a child, I recall drawing pictures of flying jets. Even though it was not the career God wanted me to have, he used my youthful desires for a short while to tell others of his truth. I enjoyed flying the small twin-engine T-37 jet trainer, yet the thrill soon wore off, and I realized it was not the career meant for me. After a while, I missed my family and I missed home. I missed my wife who was in pharmacy school at the time. It was a great experience as God allowed me to fulfill one of my childhood dreams yet it was not where God ultimately wanted me to stay. I was proud to continue serving my country in the Air Force Ready Reserve, and this allowed me to return to the beautiful hills of West Virginia. Many thought I had lost my mind to hang up my flight helmet and parachute for a coal miner's hard hat in the rugged hills of West Virginia. Again, as I look back at this great experience, I had many conversations with those seeking answers that only the Word of God could give. My Sunday school class back home had given me a beautiful Bible just before I left for Officer School. I was chosen to lead the church services while in Officer School and I used that Bible for those services. There was an atheist there who seemed like he was moving to the light of God. I witnessed to him, and just before our graduation, I gave him that Bible with a note. I truly believe it was the first Bible this man ever received. Always consider those you meet in your journey through life. It is no coincidence that you are where you are right now. Many have been brought into your life to teach you something, or they have been brought into your life to learn from you. It has definitely been a two-way street in my life as there have been many sent into my path who have encouraged and strengthened me. I certainly have appreciated their fellowship and encouragement throughout the years.

Go after it. Enjoy life as much as you can, but never forget to shed God's light and truth. If you have it, share it; if you are lacking, get it while it is available. We are the minority on this earth as most folks reject us and the love of God. They shoot us in the back with the sharp arrows of their tongues, but we must love them and be kind to those who despise us. Many folks dislike God's children and actually have no idea why (2 Peter 3:3–7). **Knowing this first, that there shall come in the last days scoffers, walking after their own lusts, and saying, "Where is the promise of his coming? for since the fathers fell asleep, all things continue as they were from the beginning of the creation." For this they willingly are ignorant of, that by the word of God the heavens were of old, and the earth standing out of the water and in the water: whereby the world that then was, being overflowed with water, perished: but the heavens and the earth, which are now, by the same word are kept in store, reserved unto fire against the day of judgment and perdition of ungodly men."**

We, as believers, yearn for the day when we are all together in the Kingdom of God. God uses us now throughout a hostile world to be witnesses of his truth and messengers of his salvation. It is our desire and prayer that his kingdom in heaven be brought down to earth forevermore. I assure you, my friend, that day will come. There is no better hope than this. The old majority in masses will be taken under the earth while we enjoy eternity in indescribable joy!

If you enjoy this life as a Christian, just imagine what God has in store during the next one! If you hate this life, then think of the joy of being rid of all the pain, the hurt, and all the wrongs for a beautiful new beginning that never ends. It is hard to accept that, at times, we feel like we are being neglected from blessings when we are actually being prepared for them.

I have often wondered how I could inspire those within the family of God as well as those outside the family to draw nearer to Him. I realized that I just simply could not accomplish such a task. I cannot inspire anyone to read or understand the Word of God or the message God is revealing to us in this book. This is because only the Holy Spirit of God can accomplish this as He speaks to you. As he alone is the *Comforter* who encourages and enables me to write, he is also the one who draws mankind's quest for God. Jesus Christ sent us the Holy Spirit after he ascended into heaven, and this Spirit comforts us, encourages us, and enables us through our struggles as we journey throughout life.

The Holy Spirit is anxiously awaiting to comfort, indwell and comfort those who turn and grasp the hand of God. Therefore, always be mindful of the underlying reason that you are reading this book—it is the Holy Spirit of God urging you to read and to move closer to God as our days are growing short. Truly following God is having faith in his Word, and your actions then reflect your faith in God. His Word provides hope, joy, and peace that is unrivaled by anything or anyone, living or dead.

For some, it may be your last opportunity before your fate is sealed. I have been called by God to feed his sheep and to seek the lost sheep, who are seeking the Shepherd. Absolute peace and security are ultimately what mankind desires at the end of the day. Those hopes are either secured or lost when they are delivered to eternity. Always keep in mind that after it is all said and done, all that is done is said. Somewhere in your life, it is recorded in heaven that you *accepted and honored God*, or it is recorded that you *rejected and dishonored* his Holy name. The result of this decision is writing the rest of the book of your life. Your life is a result of this enormous and fateful decision. Listen to wisdom.

This book cumulates a life of sixty years of experiences, trials, relationships, mountains, and valleys that are real. I have personally seen the hand of God at work in my life as well as in the lives of many others around me. God has always had a sense of humor when calling many imperfect people to his ministry, and I am certainly no exception. God never changes as I have fallen and failed many times, yet the Lord's hand has always lifted me back up and strengthened me. I get up and move on as his Spirit is my strength.

Never—and I say again, never—in this book do I intend to bring any recognition to myself. This book is not about me as it is all about *Him*. Its purpose is to honor each person taking the time to read it as God honors and loves you. I also want to lift his name above all other names and to honor God in this writing. It is my prayer that this book will touch the hearts of many and will turn their hearts to God as their walk, their talk, their close friends, and their checkbooks all reveal a heart truly separated from God. If this book helps only one get closer and to turn to his saving grace, then it has been worth all the countless 3:00+ a.m. wake-up calls from God to get this book completed. There is just something about the early morning hours that refreshes the mind so that we may enjoy God without interruption. The next time you are awakened in the early morning hours, get up and grab your Bible as God is wanting to have fellowship with you. Read the book of John and the Psalms in the early morning hours.

There are events, stories, and experiences we all tend to keep in our memories, some good and some not so good. Yet these things are to always be remembered and kept in your heart.

There was a day when God wanted to share himself with others who could relate to him and have fellowship with him, thus God desired a *family* to love, to fellowship with, and to provide for; *remember that day.*

There was a day when God created the heavens and the earth; *remember that day.*

There was a day when God created man and woman; *remember that day.*

There was a day when man rebelled against God, and eternal life with his Creator was lost and was replaced with spiritual and eventual physical death. While the earth was filled with the light and glory of God, there was now a sea of darkness which engulfed the earth. The earth and mankind were now cursed due to man's sin; *remember that day.*

There was a day when God's plan to restore man to his original position with Him would be implemented, thus *the plan of salvation* began; *remember that day.*

There was a day that mankind became so evil that God sought out and saved the only family who truly loved Him and destroyed all the living things upon the earth; *remember that day.*

There was a day when God delivered the nation of Israel from the bondage of Egypt and provided a way to the Promised Land; *remember that day.*

There was a day when God sent his Son to earth to complete his plan of saving mankind, and through Abraham, Isaac, Jacob, and David came God in the flesh, Jesus Christ. Born of a virgin, now God with us was on the earth to dwell with mankind; *remember that day.*

There was a day that the Son of God was crucified, died, and arose again the third day. Now the light was shown to all and salvation made available to anyone who would receive it; *remember that day.*

There will be a day when the Son of God returns to receive his own and to take them to their new home in heaven. The new home which will descend from heaven back to our new earth; *live for this day.*

There will be a day when the King of kings and Lord of lords will return, with his army, to earth and rescue Israel and defeat her enemies; *live for this day.*

There will be a day when all those who truly loved God and his Son will live and reign on earth for all eternity. The glory of the *Lord* shall fill the earth, and we will live in eternal peace and joy. *Live for this day.*

There will be a day when all who have rejected the love of God and his means of salvation will face eternal and final judgment; *don't live for this day.*

There will be a day when all the governments of evil and those who served them will be cast into eternal darkness where the soul never dies; *don't live for this day.*

There will be a day when eternal misery begins in the darkness of hell where peace, light, and joy are no longer attainable, but regret, darkness, and suffering will be unbearable for all imprisoned there.

Those who refused God's hand will have no hope, no choice, and no appeals as their new eternal home is established; *don't live for this day.*

There will be a day when the new earth will be filled with the glory of God as He enjoys fellowship with His people; *live for this day*.

Today is the day of salvation, and the Creator of heaven and earth is calling all to come home, my child, it's suppertime. There is a place setting for everyone born upon this earth at the table in heaven. It will be the most important meal you'll ever be invited to—the marriage supper of the Lamb. Don't throw away your invitation. There is *absolutely* nothing more valuable than your name being written in the Lamb's Book of Life. *Nothing*. Your invitation expires upon death.

We are now living in a crucial time in human and biblical history as we are clearly living in the latter days, as prophesied in the Holy Scriptures. I will not join those who predict the exact time of the end of the age nor the return of Christ. However, I will tell you that *everything* is in place scripturally for *his imminent return*. Normalcy may never be back, but the Son of God surely will. The events of our time, the technological advances, and the world governments are now perfectly in place for the final cleansing and judgment of mankind to begin and Israel's redemption to take place. This is what the Book of Revelation is all about—the cleansing of the earth, God completing His final wrath and judgment to the wicked, Israel's final redemption, and ushering in the Lord of lords and King of kings to rule the earth.

Please take heed, my friend, there is nothing more urgent in your life right now than to prepare for *Christ's imminent return*. The Bible has been remarkably accurate in all it's prophecy, and I assure you the rest of it will come to pass and could happen in our lifetime. It must be noted that God declares the end at the beginning (Isaiah 46:9–10). He reveals this to us to assure those who truly place their faith and trust in Him need not to worry about their welfare. Romans 8:28 assures us that "**All things work together to the good of those that love the Lord and are called according to His purpose.**"

For all of those seeking a way to find God's will, I'll give you the answer: Love the true living God with your all. That's it. Now you have recognized the mess you've made in life trying to fly in the dark skies alone. Yet you are in a graveyard spiral; but hopefully you've handed the yoke over to God. He will level the wings and change the attitude and altitude of your aircraft (life). A decision to turn the controls over to a much more qualified pilot will take you safely home. He and he alone can deliver you back to blue skies, and my, how blue they are! When you truly love God, you will fully trust him and your deliverance is forever secured.

Despite all our storms in life, He and He alone will sustain and deliver us. He owns the cattle on a thousand hills, and he sees even a sparrow as it falls. Thus, this book was written to educate, inform, and encourage those searching for a better understanding of God's message in these challenging and latter days. Many fine people have suffered due to the coronavirus, and many ask if this was a judgment of God. Drastic events and tragedies on earth usually result in mankind questioning God and their position with Him. During such events of plagues, weather, earthquakes, etc., man will either turn toward God and seek his face or rebel and sink deeper and deeper into the sea of darkness. It is unfortunate and heartbreaking to have seen so many innocent people suffering and dying from this awful disease. Again, we initiated all of this imperfect world in the Garden of Eden, and from there we shaped an imperfect and hazardous environment. This environment is unfortunately influenced by spiritual forces that rebel against God and his family.

In this fallen world and in our darkest times, however, we must look beyond the devastating effects of the virus and place our faith and trust in God to deliver us. God has placed plagues and pestilences on earth in the past due to excessive sin and disobedience by mankind. He may or may not have sent this virus, but the virus pandemic will draw many closer to him, and those whose lives were put on hold now have a chance to reevaluate their position with our Creator. I cannot overemphasize the urgency to heed the call of God. To grasp his hand initially for some; to grasp it tighter for others. These pestilences and series of earthquakes and storms are more signs that we are truly living in the last days prophesized in the Bible.

There are no politics in the kingdom of heaven, as Jesus said, "You are either for me or against me." When all the layers of intellectual, spiritual, prideful, and boastful clothing are stripped from mankind, we must face the reality that we are all naked and equal. We were born this way, and we will die this way. Everything we have in between was given to us. That's right, *everything*. The events of the coronavirus have brought this point to us loud and clear. It has taken the young, the old, the rich, and the poor. I deeply appreciate the love and sacrifices made by so many health-care workers and first responders as many have given their lives to save others. What love these heroes bestowed. My deepest appreciation goes to all those who gave some and to those who gave all.

Our lives are viewed in heaven and earth as either a pond or a stream. Some lives are like a stagnant pond, as some hoard all they can in life and thus build their own pond of riches that never flows to anyone else. Some lives are like streams of fresh water running to others, as their blessings are shared to those around them (John 7:37–39). Did you buy up all the N95 masks and never shared one with your neighbor that worked the ambulance crew? A quick glance at your checkbook will reveal the true intentions of your heart. A meticulous accounting record is kept in heaven of every dime you have made and spent while on earth. Have you supported your church? Have you supported sending the Word of God to all the nations of the earth? Have you fed the hungry? Have you clothed the poor? My mother once said and said it well, "The only thing you take to heaven is what you gave away on earth."

At the end of this book, one point will be made clear—you are within the flock or you are without. If you are without the flock, you are without hope, peace, joy, wisdom, understanding, clothing, food, water, a home, friends, mercy, forgiveness, love, and most of all God, as everyone in the pit of darkness can verify. Now is the time to get within the flock as the Chief Shepherd, Jesus Christ, is calling you to green pastures. His hand is still there for you. He will pull you into his ship of safety, that old ship of Zion.

I once witnessed to a man that worked outside at the coal mine in Ohio. I would take time usually at the end of the day to witness to this man. Then one day, he said to me," Jamie, you don't know just what all I have done."

My reply was quick as I replied, "I don't care what you have done, and neither does God, as he will forgive *all* of your sin." For those of you who are not in the family of God, you must focus not on what you have done wrong in your past but on what you can do *right* for the remainder of your life. Understanding-ably some have more sins to cover than others, but all sin comes short of the righteousness of Christ yet his blood is sufficient to cleanse all our sin. So move while you have the ability. My mother quoted one of her favorite scriptures not long before her death, and it was so appropriate for all of us,

> **"Therefore have I hope. It is of the LORD'S mercies that we are not consumed, because his compassions fail not. They are new every morning, great is thy faithfulness"** (Lamentations 3.21–23).

I am pleased to report that individual at the coal mine later turned his life over to the Lord *and is* now in heaven. I was not the means but the messenger. God provides the means for eternal life, and all other false religions provide the means to eternal death. This book points to our Father and his Son being the *only* means to eternal salvation.

I also am reminded of a close friend who, at the age of fifty, told me that he had just a few months left to live. His name was Bruce Dean, a state of Ohio mine inspector. I include his name as I know he would want me to. He was not a good man; He was a great man to those who knew him. I had witnessed to Bruce as well as other state and federal inspectors while working in Ohio. One day, I had one of those phone calls we all dread from Bruce. "I have terminal cancer, Jamie," were the words that brought tears to my eyes as I drove down Route 33 in Albany, Ohio.

This close friend spilled his guts to me, and it was a heart-wrenching phone call to say the least. Bruce stated on the call that "you don't have to be a good man, nor a great man but a saved man." He knew he had lived a good life, but he needed to be saved. That he did as he prayed the sinner's prayer on the phone that very day. He then quickly said he wanted to make the best of what life he had left to lead others to the Lord, and that time was only a few months.

What a testimony this guy had, and what a story to tell of one fine man who now sits in the glory of heaven. He instantly wanted to give as soon as he received such a gift from God. As I considered the detrimental effects of the coronavirus, I thought of one of my friends last statements, "I am one of the lucky ones, Jamie. I now know that I will be dying soon, and now I can be saved and be right with God. I could have been hit head-on by a coal truck and never had that chance."

Countless souls have contracted the deadly virus, and many have died as a result. However, the pause in their lives due to contracting the virus may have changed their eternal destiny. Which of the two are of most value? It is truly heart-wrenching to mourn the loss of a loved one. No words can describe the feelings we experience when a loved one leaves this earth. Yet, there is peace in knowing that they are now safe and no longer suffering but walking the streets paved of gold. I will see my friend Bruce again someday, as well as many others who have gone before me, in the family of God.

While this book was written to encourage all readers to evaluate their priorities, it was also written to motivate those spiritually equipped servants of God to get off the couch and fulfill the task given to us by our Lord Jesus Christ. How many adults do you see having a meal with milk bottles? Sadly many lifelong Christians are nearing the end of their lives still drinking from a milk bottle. It will be quite embarrassing when our reward comes in heaven as hay and stubble. Who wants to get to the gates of glory by the skin of our teeth? Mature believers must no longer look at Jesus as a small babe lying in a manger, but He is now presiding in great majesty, being the King of kings and Lord of lords. With great boldness and excitement, we must be proclaiming His truth and the coming of His Kingdom!

We must get into the meat and the good food God has for us so that we may grow and that others may know the truth—the truth that sets us free. The fairness and justness of God requires all to have his truth revealed to each and every person. This process of fairness includes the roles of those who have been forgiven and freed from sin.

We must redeem the time as our hourglass reveals that our time to make a difference is running short. There are so many out there who needs encouragement, hope, and peace in their lives. You can see it everywhere if you will only take the time to look and listen. Our gifts of experiences, our education, and priceless treasures of wisdom are all useless if contained within oneself. Now we will begin our first journey in the Book of Genesis.

# Chapter 1

## A Journey in Genesis: A Miracle in the Desert

**And Abraham called the name of his son that was born unto him, whom Sarah bare to him, Isaac. And Abraham circumcised his son Isaac being eight days old, as God had commanded him.**

The master plan of God is unquestionably the most important truth we must understand. First of all, it is made easy to understand. Many scholars and highly educated theologians have made God's master plan difficult to understand. However, we must make one point on this introduction, and it is this: if there is a one true sovereign God, then we must assume that he would:

A)  Want all to know him and his plan for humanity.
B)  Provide a means for his plan to be known
C)  Define and expose those who work against His will and just how important and precious each soul on earth actually is. You must understand, the enemy is strong and deceitful, and most fall into his deception.
D)  Define the destiny and rewards to those who *accept* his plan and to those who *reject* Him and his plan.

It is God's deepest desire for you to know him as well as his plan for you. He uses his chosen messengers, his angels, his Spirit, and his Word to make his plan known to all of humanity.

We are so privileged to live in a time where we have the complete Word of God (Holy Bible) at our disposal in all major parts of the world. While it is restricted in many countries, it still thrives and is cherished in the underground church. The Internet has also been a blessing in that the Bible can be viewed and/or downloaded with a mere click of a button.

For all of the critics out there of the Holy Bible, simply use the common sense God has given you in this profound assumption: if there is truly only one true, sovereign God, then wouldn't it be reasonable to assume that his Word and his message would be known above all other religions? Of course it would. There is no other book that comes close to the number of Bibles published throughout the world. There is no other book that has truly moved and influenced so many souls. It is estimated that five to six billion copies exist worldwide. This does not include those that are copied in the underground church and those kept on computers and iPhone storages.

Another assumption that is simple and clear is that all other religious books do not answer the deep questions we all have about ourselves. Such questions as, how did I get here on this planet that is spinning one thousand miles per hour and rotating around the sun at sixty-seven thousand miles per hour? How is it spinning so smoothly and consistently? Also how did this perfect environment of life ever come into existence? I'm sure God laughs at us as we spend countless resources drilling the earth and flying the universe searching answers for our origin. He made all things, and he did it in six days. The history of mankind is approximately six thousand years old. While science is great, it is useless if you don't begin with design being at the forefront. With all things working so perfectly on earth and above the earth, we should never question the one who designed it and then created it.

While humanity struggles in making real progress of our origin, we focus too much on what we don't know and neglect the all-knowing Creator of all things. God is real, and we have real science as a result. Beware of the deceiver and his deception. We should all be impressed, amazed, and thankful for such a creation. This reality doesn't take a great deal of intelligence; it just takes common sense.

Also consider just how did this perfect body that has emotions, memory, and reasoning ever come into existence? There is absolutely nothing like our perfectly made body among the living creatures. Nothing.

Have you ever seen a herd of deer conducting a funeral service at the roadside when a family member lies dead beside the road? With such a perfect body living in such a perfect environment, one must carefully consider the question, "Why am I here?" Listen to your heart and use common sense when considering our origin and our purpose. The road to disprove the true God is difficult to construct, but our adversary relentlessly tries to devise and convince us humans of his lie. It is not only a road to his destruction, but it's wide pathway takes the majority of mankind to the pits of hell. Science and technology have their place in society as long as they ultimately point to the awesome power and knowledge of our Creator.

Perhaps the greatest answer the Bible gives humanity is how to deal with the guilt we all have inborn within us. Guilt we consciously possess by being born in a sinful state of rebelling against God. Just consider, for a moment, of all the world's religions that exist that are simply trying to deal with this guilt (while they are all failing). Man has an inherit deep vacuum within his soul which can only be filled by his Creator. However, our Creator is holy, pure, and has been separated from man due to his rebellion. This sin (disobedience to God) was solely man's misstep in the Garden of Eden. No other religion truly answers the way we can deal with this deep loss of fellowship with God (vacuum) within ourselves but through faith in the true living God.

We have discussed these topics earlier as emphasis must be made on the truth of the Bible as well as our origin. The archeological evidence of the Bible is overwhelming and unrivaled by any other religion. Historians have often used the Holy Bible as a reference in researching our history. How appropriate. The Bible ends just as it begins—God with man, on earth, enjoying each other. However, in the 783,137 words of the Bible, we find billions of souls in between and you being one of those souls. While you have just a moment now on planet earth, you must utilize what time you have left for the Kingdom of God. Each and every soul is precious to God, and he yearns to have fellowship with *you*. The Good Shepherd would leave the flock of ninety-nine and even give his life to save the one lost sheep. As we hear his call, we must seek him, and he will lead us to safety and to green pastures, he will lead us beside the still waters.

Again, remember that the body just happens to be the shell that the soul and spirit of man dwells in. Man is a soul and spirit that lives in the body. Yes, the bodies we now have will die, and God has promised to give us all that place their faith in him a new body. A new body that never dies in a beautiful new earth, with our Creator, is the desire of God and should be your utmost desire. Yet, let us return to the billions of souls previously mentioned who are and have been upon this earth. The Bible makes it perfectly clear that *all* of mankind will live forever, and it is up to *each* individual as to where he spends eternity. It is not God's choice but yours.

The final solution of God's adversary is to deceive, dispute, and utterly destroy God's truth and those of his who are called, chosen, and faithful. The Bible assures us that the victory over evil has been won as we will see in the following twenty-three chapters. The fight for your soul begins as a child, and Satan is relentless to deceive you from the truth and to derail all those who are on track following and serving God. Many must overcome the deceit of childhood influence to permanently alter our way of perceiving life. Many have never been taken to church, never heard nor read the messages revealed in the Bible, and have been mistreated, abused, and neglected most of their lives. They have lived a life of drowning in the dark sea of sin and ignorance. Always remember, the hand of God will pull you out of this deceitful constant dwelling in the past Satan throws up to you. God will never let go of your hand.

Satan minimizes the love God has bestowed upon all of us, but he cannot fully quench the abundance of this love. Satan then moves to fill the desires of self, and promising rewards that ultimately separates us from intimate fellowship with God.

Remember, Satan is powerful and manipulative, and his tools of pride, discouragement, envy, and selfish desires are the ones he uses most. He's either trying to convince you that you have never been important to anyone or that you are the most important person to everyone. Make no mistake about it, God is a god of the future and it is a bright future. Satan is a god of the past. He constantly regrets his past as his pride and arrogance recklessly destined him to an eternal hell that he knows will be his destiny. It is his goal to take as many souls as he can with him, so don't live in the past. Every day is a bright and new day for those living in the family of God. Yes, many will be in pain, many will stumble, and many will fall. But they will get back up, for there is joy in the morning to all those who love and seek God.

Now we shall begin our journey of how God plans to restore the relationship lost in the Garden of Eden when Adam and Eve were deceived and disobeyed God. This act, seeming to be small, separated man from God.

God's plan for man's redemption was a simple one in definition, but was very profound when considering the cost. So in definition, the remedy was a mere sacrifice made to God to forever rid our sin in his eyes. Simply we get a lamb, sacrifice it to the *Lord*, and all is good on planet Earth. Not quite. It had to be a lamb without blemish. It had to be spotless. It had to be totally innocent. The hard part was that man had to sin no more after the sacrifice or another sacrifice would have to be made. So God's plan was this,

> **"For God so loved the world, that he gave his only begotten Son, that whosoever believeth in him should not perish, but have everlasting life"** (John 3:16).

This is the profound part, my friend. There cannot be enough books written, searches made by the finest men of God, or any way to measure the tremendous cost it would take to *totally cleanse* our filth from God's record. Sacrifices of untold number were made to *cover* man's sins, but God's finished work would include a sacrifice that *cleansed* all our sins once and for all. Yet it was his plan, and what a plan it was. While it was a plan that confused many, we can see it so clearly now, and what a joy it is to share such a treasure to all those living today.

To begin God's plan, he would choose a faithful man whose family would be blessed into twelve tribes and then into a nation and ultimately, into a kingdom. Through this family would multitudes be born and blessed as the number of the stars and the sands of the sea. Through this family would the nations be blessed that blessed them, and those who cursed them would also be cursed. Through this family, the world would know without a doubt the god of their fathers would be God of heaven and earth. Through this family would God's nature and his heart be revealed as well as his plan for all of humanity. It would involve two thousand years of captivity, man-appointed judges, priests and kings before the Savior would come who would free us from all bondage, from all captivity, and be a righteous Judge, Priest and the true King of all kings and Lord of lords.

So, to begin all of this journey, God chose a man named Abram (later named Abraham) to be the father of all nations, and through him, all nations would be blessed. "**And he believed in the Lord; and he counted it to him for righteousness**" (Genesis 15:6). It should be noted that the main requirement mentioned in the Bible is that Abraham had faith in God. When you truly possess faith in something, then action must reinforce that faith. He saw immediately that God was real, and his spirit and soul moved toward this wonderful God of truth.

God told Abraham to pack his bags and leave his home in Haran (Ur) to a land God would give him and his descendants. At the age of seventy-five, he left his home and began his journey. So was the miracle in the desert the fact that a seventy-five-year-old man would leave his comfort zone to an unknown journey to an unknown land? I do know that it would take a miracle for me to do that! The miracle in the desert was a bit more, and it was for one reason—to prove God would be faithful in keeping his Word and that only God could cause a child to be born in such a miraculous fashion. It would be another two thousand years later that another miraculous childbirth would change eternity and mankind forever.

How amazing it is to consider how the barren wombs of many women became the means to keep God's promise to Israel. Without the barren women Sarah, Rebekah, Rachel, Hannah, and Elizabeth, we would never have heard of Isaac, Jacob, Joseph, Samuel, and John the Baptist. We must realize we have no hope in this barren world without a sovereign, omniscient, omnipresent, and loving God to intervene. While Sarah was the first to experience this intervention of the barren, we see the same pattern throughout Israel's history. This pattern reveals humanity's need for God to deliver us from a barren land to the promised land. Some may call these childbirths miraculous, and some may call them by divine intervention. Abraham and Sarah needed some serious help regardless of what one may call it.

Abraham and Sarah needed a miracle as Sarah was too old to have a child. Abraham was one hundred years old and Sarah was ninety when she conceived. God gave them a son, and his name was Isaac. The name means "laughter," as Sarah and Abraham laughed at God when he said she would have a child in her old age. Another example of proving Abraham's faith when God asked him to sacrifice Isaac when he was a young boy. Isaac was placed on an altar and about to be killed, when an angel of God appeared and stopped him. Isaac was saved as God provided a ram that Abraham found caught in the bushes. This was a foreshadow of things to come as God's plan would become clear as we read on. A sacrifice would have to be provided by God that could actually *cleanse* us from all of our unrighteousness. Isaac had the son, Jacob, of whom the twelve tribes of Israel would be born. It should be noted that the Old Testament and its purpose cannot be underestimated as not only is it great for historic significance, but it is rich in substance that God wants all to know. While it, at times, is difficult to read and understand, just remember that God is holy, and we chose not to be holy in the Garden of Eden. Thereupon, God implemented a plan to restore us to holiness, and it was his plan, not ours. The master plan addresses all people who have ever or will ever exist upon the face of the earth. It is only appropriate that the Creator of all things not only establishes a plan of redemption but explains it to those involved. We are so privileged to be living on earth at this time. As we continue on our journey, we will see what God has in store for those who truly seek him with their heart, soul, and spirit. His reward to those who seek him cannot possibly be described in it's entirety nor can the suffering and anguish those are experiencing in the pits of hell.

The plan God made with his chosen nation, Israel, was not just for them but for all, as we discover throughout our journey. There should never be any criticism of the Jewish faith and the nation of Israel. While they are looking now for a Messiah who has already come, the Jewish Nation will be the center of attention to God, Satan, and the entire world as the end of the age draws near. The world stage is set for their final redemption and call from God to accept the true Messiah. The call, my friend, goes not only to them but to every soul on earth. Seek him now where he can be found and rest *in him*. We should pray for peace in Jerusalem as it is the desire of our heavenly Father and peace will ultimately come to pass just as he promised.

In the "Miracle in the Desert," we see how the God of Abraham, Isaac, and Jacob would keep his word to a man of faith. It will be a pattern we see throughout our journey and we can rely on today. We will see throughout our journey that God keeps his word.

# CHAPTER 2

## A Journey in the Book of Exodus: In the Shadow of Bondage

**And the people stood afar off, and Moses drew near unto the thick darkness where God was. And the Lord said unto Moses, "Thus thou shalt say unto the children of Israel, Ye have seen that I have talked with you from heaven.**

This scripture (verses 21–22) of chapter 20 takes us from the family of Abraham to a man named Moses. This story is about bondage and the need of a savior. God foretold Abraham before he died that his descendants would be in captivity for four hundred years, and they would be bound in slavery under the Egyptians for four centuries. There has been some debate comparing Egyptian history to Biblical history as there has simply been a small discretion in date setting. The chronology of the Bible is correct, and again, be aware that our adversary wants to distort the truth in any way to create confusion and doubt in the minds of mankind. Remember, my friend, you are the prey. The Word of God is true.

In this journey, we will be introduced to God's chosen people who have been in bondage for four hundred years and were in bad need of a savior. God's Word was again kept true as we see seventy members of Abraham's family who went into Egypt for safety and food now has grown to over two million people. The family's entry into Egypt was welcomed at the beginning, as we see one of Jacob's sons, Joseph finds favor in the eyes of Pharaoh.

Joseph's story was an interesting one as his brothers were historically jealous of him. The brothers sold Joseph into slavery after Jacob had sent Joseph to check on the brothers. Joseph later interpreted a dream of Pharaoh which not only preserved the family of Jacob, but Pharaoh's kingdom as well. Joseph revealed that there would be seven years of feast, as the land would produce plenty in harvest, followed by seven years of famine. He placed Joseph next to him in all the land and led the Egyptian nation in preserving food for seven years and then surviving through the next seven years of famine. God always forewarns mankind before he places judgment upon the earth. In this case, a king recognized the authority of God through Jacob's son Joseph and responded and respected these people. It would be a trend for *all governments* and *all people* to take heed to, "Bless God's people and be blessed or curse God's people and be cursed" (Genesis 12). The end result was not only Jacob's family being blessed but the entire land of Egypt as well.

While the seven years of abundance of food and wine was enjoyable, those aware knew seven years of famine were coming, and they were prepared. It was perhaps the seven years of famine that many realized the God of Jacob and his son Joseph was the true God, and through him, many lives were preserved. As many events in the Bible are shadows of things to come, we must consider the thought that this same event, in greater magnitude, will occur again. If the stock market is any indicator of prosperity, the last six to seven years have been the most prosperous in our history. The market has grown over seventeen thousand points in the last seven years. America and the world have been "storing the corn and grain" during this time as our 401(k) plans reveal. However, it is just a matter of time until the seven years of famine will ravage the earth and its inhabitants. The judgment and wrath of God will come at a time that most will never expect (Matthew 24). This story of Joseph and Egypt is a mere foreshadowing of the seven-year tribulation period described both in the book of Daniel and the book of Revelation. Careful study reveals Joseph is a form of Christ to Israel. Many times, we realize that the painting of God's master plan is completed as we have seen in past events. His plan for all of us was laid out so carefully onto a canvas outline back before creation of earth was made. Then he carefully paints them in as some events seem smaller while they get larger as time goes on. The canvas is almost completed, and very little is left to be painted in as the end of the age is drawing so close.

It is a canvas now that we can all see patterns of the past leading up to the last days or the day of Jacob's trouble. We have seen on this canvas great amounts of war and famine and pestilences (plagues, viruses, etc.), but this time is the big one, as billions of souls will perish in the last days (Revelation 9:18). Earlier, the canvas had illustrated the earth being cleansed with water by God, yet the final cleansing will be even greater but this time by fire. The canvas was painted with so many chosen of God proclaiming the truth and salvation of God which pointed to a King coming into Jerusalem on an ass. Yet there is a place on the canvas where that King returns to earth with all of his faithful to defeat all forces of evil and the world governments, which have ruled the earth for thousands of years. This book has no value to God nor to man if it doesn't add to that number of those riding behind the Lord of lords and King of kings on that day. Be in that faithful army. (Revelation chapters 17 and 19).

Again I must emphasize that everything is in place as the Bible has foretold for the end of the age to come to pass. It must be considered that the Son of God will return for those who "love his appearing" at a time when those upon the earth least expect it. However, the second coming of Christ in all his glory and with his saints can be well timed as it will happen three and a half years after the temple has been desecrated by the Antichrist. The departure of the bride will be a time that no man knoweth but the Father only. Christ will come after his bride. He will come at an hour that will be sudden and a shock to most of humanity. Normalcy will exist when the departure of the church occurs as no man knoweth the day or the hour. Jesus said it will simply be a normal day as folks are getting married, drinking, and having a good time just as the days were in Noah's time. Christ's arrival on earth with his army of faithful saints and holy angels will be a well predicted time as it will occur three and a half years after the

Antichrist desecrates the temple. There are two distinct time periods here as you carefully study the books of Daniel and Revelation.

Now let's get back to Moses and a new Pharaoh that had forgotten all the benefits and prosperity that had come from Jacob's family.

There is so much to discuss when we journey through the books of Moses as he wrote the first five books of the Old Testament. This guy was special to God, to say the least. So special that God physically spoke to Moses and talked directly with him while leading God's people out of the bondage of Egypt to the Promised Land. He was also so special that Jesus took Peter, James, and John upon a mountain and showed himself in his glory, with Moses and Elijah, to his disciples. That was something very special!

God also buried Moses. Just as the entire world needed a savior to redeem mankind, Israel was a shadow of the world in need of a Savior. The Pharaoh of Joseph's day honored Jacob's family and blessed them generously. Yet this Pharaoh died, and Israel was not favored in the eyes of the new ruler. In fact, he mistakenly and fatefully thought Israel would be a threat to Egyptian rule as they multiplied greatly in the land of Egypt. The more they prospered and multiplied, the harsher Pharaoh became on them as they became the slaves of Egypt.

This imagery of enslavement as well as mankind all being in a sea of darkness both presents the state of Israel as well as the state of mankind. There is nothing more troubling than one rushing from childhood through a short life of seventy to one hundred years not contemplating his end. Our end is just our beginning. We all mourn the death of loved ones, and we all need to. However, always remember, no one truly dies (speaking of your soul and spirit). The closer we examine this reality, the more we should emphasize our true position and how we can enhance that position. It is an inherent trait God gave us to want to better ourselves, and there is nothing wrong that. However, it is when obsession sets in that leads to idolizing things of no value compared to things of eternal value. We weigh these values *every day*. The land of Egypt, as well as the rest of the world, had their share of false gods and idols that couldn't speak, couldn't save, and couldn't provide anything of value to Israel or anyone else. Yet we will see their demise as history and the bible records Israel's path of obedience and disobedience as they journeyed to the promised land.

Whatever happened to the mighty Egyptian Empire? Where are all the Pharaohs? Amazingly, we now see Israel back as a prosperous nation and the promises God made to Abraham, Isaac, and Jacob are standing as a solid rock that nothing can move. God definitely has a sense of humor as he chose such a tiny little patch of real estate for him and his people to reside in. He could have chosen an entire continent as he owns it all. While the humility of God and his Son is beyond comprehension, it is a likeness that they seek in those that love them (James 4:6).

The idols and false gods that Israel were exposed to would prove to be detrimental as Moses came to deliver them out of their four hundred years of bondage. We should carefully consider the question as to why did they have to suffer so long, being they were the chosen by such a powerful God? The sea of darkness and the state of man since our fall in the Garden of Eden cannot be described. It has to be experienced. The deliverance from such bondage and darkness also has to be lived and experienced. Great was the offence. Great were the consequences. Great was the remedy to restore. The slavery they were subjected to for four hundred years could be in direct parallel with the slavery we all are born into this world and that is sin. Again the canvas added some color to this great darkness and the deliverance of God's people. The canvas will again add tremendous color when all the saints and elect of God have been delivered to the Promised Land on this new earth. What an artist we have here!

God takes us to Mount Sinai on this journey as he has joyfully delivered his people from the slavery of Egypt. Can you imagine the Red Sea parting and allowing God's people to walk on dry ground? Can you imagine the joy of witnessing Pharaoh and his army being destroyed by the sea collapsing over them as they pursued the Jewish people? God delivered his people as an eagle carries her young to safety. What a beautiful image. This protection is still available to all who seek him. Now God instructs Moses to place a boundary around the mountain as God himself will be coming down to Mount Sinai. The Glory of God had to be an amazing though terrifying experience for all of Israel to behold. God wanted all of Israel to know that Moses was his chosen leader. He was led by God to reveal His plans and rules to His chosen people. God spoke directly to Moses, and we begin to see God instructing his people as he gives Moses the Ten Commandments on the top of Mount Sinai.

We won't go into great detail on Ten Commandments, yet we clearly see in the scriptures before and after 20:22 that God wants *all* to know that he wants to be *the* God of their lives, not one of many. He commands them early not to serve anything made of gold or silver or any image but to serve him and him only. His Son would later reveal the greatest commandment of all, and that was "Thou shalt love the Lord thy God with all of thy heart, with all of thy soul and with all of thy spirit. There is no greater commandment than this." As we continue in our journey to the book of Leviticus, we recognize the more of the holiness of God, and emphasis will be made on the second greatest commandment, "Thy shalt love thy neighbor as thyself." If there was one theme that could be made for the entire Bible, it would be just that simple—Love God with your *all*, and then share that love with *all* those you encounter.

It's some of what you say, and it's some of what you do. But it's all of *who* you love, that truly defines you.

# Chapter 3

## A Journey in the Book of Leviticus: A Holy God

> **And if a man shall take his brother's wife, it is an unclean thing: he hath uncovered his brother's nakedness; they shall be childless. Ye shall therefore keep all my statues, and all my judgements and do them: that the land, whither I bring you to dwell therein, spue you not out.**

In Genesis, we see that we, as mere humans, erred in such a seemingly small way (after all, it was simply eating a fruit that looked good) but had devastating results. This pattern, as previously discussed, of placing a lot of value on things of little to no value. Adam and Eve didn't see the train wreck coming. They had no idea what a tragic loss they created, not only for themselves but for all of humanity. While hindsight is always twenty twenty, we just begin to see early in the book of Genesis just how separated we are from a Holy God and how a small error on humanity's part was astronomical. While facedown in the sea of darkness, we only see darkness, yet as we turn to the light as we grab the hand of salvation, we see the light and rest in it.

> **"He sent from above, He took me out of many waters"** (2 Samuel 22:17).

We move on to Exodus, and we see the called people of God now delivered from slavery, and Israel has made a tabernacle for God to dwell in. Isn't it again a huge example of humility to see the creator of the universe dwelling in a tent?

God has also shown Israel that a blood sacrifice had to be made for the remission of sins (atonement for our sins). While some 1,400 years would pass until the ultimate sacrifice would be made once for all of mankind. Just as one man (Adam) cursed all of mankind into a fallen world, one man (Jesus Christ) would provide a means for deliverance and redemption for those who believed. Thus, no faith in Christ's sacrifice, then no hope of deliverance.

As we visited earlier, God instructed Israel on how to specifically build the tabernacle for him to dwell in, and now we have a delivered people, a place for God to dwell, and now it is time to get into the details on just how holy God was. The objective of God was to instruct his people through ceremonies and of observance and abiding by his laws, they would be sanctified through these acts. These people would be set apart by a God that was Holy. God said, "Be holy, for I am Holy." It should be noted all the ceremonies and festivals should be acknowledged to this day as a remembrance of the state we were in (as well as Israel) and where we are now (a delivered, sanctified, holy people through the finished work of Jesus Christ). Beware of the trend to rid the world of our past history as many evil folks would like to destroy all of our history that involves freedom and God.

A thorough study in God's law can take quite some time and a lot of thought. However, in Leviticus 21–22, we are placed in a time where God is giving us strict rules in one of his laws—sexual sins. We also see that in verse 22, God puts a condition to Israel to keep this law (as well as His others), or they will forfeit their right to dwell in the land God had given them.

Perhaps Satan and his demons took advantage of this stipulation as he influenced the hearts and minds of the Jews to their eventual eviction. Again, Satan is a rival to all those in the family of God as well as those seeking and contemplating a relationship with the Sovereign God. One of our enemy's greatest tools is to lure the desires of the flesh to overrule the laws of God. We have example after example in the Bible of those who had fallen to this temptation. We see a man that God said was after his own heart as king David committed not one but many sins all because he fell into temptation of sexual sin. We see this great king suffer great consequences by committing adultery and murder. He had a relationship with Bathsheba and then had her husband sent to the front lines of battle to be killed. While it is not for us to judge this man after God's own heart, we must consider how this king and favored man of God could be lured into this trap of sexual sin.

We also see Sodom and Gomorrah both being destroyed because of the sexual immorality both cities promoted. They were led by a king that had been raided and robbed, yet a man of righteousness (Abraham) had come to deliver all the king's possessions back to him. The king knew of Abraham's heritage and the God that Abraham served. Abraham's nephew Lot was a resident in the city, and I'm sure he was remembered by his uncle's heroic act for the king and the cities. Yet the sin was so great in these cities that God utterly destroyed both of them with fire and hailstones from heaven. Lot and his two daughters were rescued by angels and delivered to safety before the judgment occurred.

We also see Samson, one of the judges chosen by God, fall in love with the wrong woman (a Philistine) who deceived him to his demise. As the Philistine woman deceived him, he revealed the secret of his strength only to lose it as well as his life. The sexual sins of that day most certainly didn't disappear as our enemy continues to use his tools to derail and destroy the lives of many. His tools of deception, greed, pride, and lust are neatly redefined as subjective truth, bettering oneself, being well known, and trying to "find myself sexually." These lies to our consciousness should take us way back to the Garden of Eden and see where one small act of disobedience to God started a landslide for mankind that only God could cease. Many messengers of God have been ridiculed for their stance on sexual sins and for good reason; people love themselves more than they love God. When anyone, any book or any leader opposes their love for themselves, then they are identified as insensitive, racist, homophobic, antigay, or gay bashers. While there are some that may fall into this category, no true Christian would ever be a hater of anyone, regardless of their orientation. The same could be true in identifying the God of Abraham, Isaac, and Jacob. God, as well as his true followers, has no hatred whatsoever to any soul on earth. There is no better way to describe someone who lives the most unholy, unclean, despicable life as the one whom God loves the most. The driver (Satan) that separates us from God is our sinful nature driven both by our own selfish desires and ambitions fueled by the forces of the fallen angel, Satan.

God hates the driver, not the person. God's people despise the driver, not the person. The driver of sin simply separates us from God and the benefits of being included in his family. It is that simple. It is impossible to call anyone a father if they have consciously or subconsciously decided to live a life of disobedience to his rules. He wants you home at midnight from a date, yet you deliberately come in every weekend at 1:30 a.m. He still feeds you and clothes you and protects you despite your disobedience, but it grieves him every night as he sees your bed empty after midnight. This is how God feels about sin, yet the final penalty is when a drunk driver had been drinking at a bar all night and then drove a pickup truck over the daughter as she got out of the car on her date at 1:00 a.m. Had she been obedient, she would have been safely in bed at midnight. There is safety in knowing and obeying the Lord.

It is one thing to come in after midnight once in a blue moon yet another to totally balk at the father's authority. We have all made mistakes, yet the daughter didn't make just a single mistake. She lived a life of rebellion and was insensitive to the fathers rules. The father tried and tried to protect his beautiful daughter with simple rules, yet her constant rebellion eventually cost her life. The same analogy is true in those who truly love God will pursue him as a child follows his father. Many on earth have been blessed with a good father, while some have not or simply never had one. Yet there is a Father above that is worlds apart from the best earthly fathers, and he is there for all who seek him.

We never know what battles our fellow men are facing as many so-called Christians spend way too much time criticizing and belittling others. It is not for any of us to judge any soul on earth as only God knows the heart of man. It is not our right nor our role to judge others. It is our role to tell others to follow Christ as he forgives and cleanses us from all uncleanliness and places us in the family of God.

Therefore, be fully aware while there is chastisement to those who stray for the believer, there is judgment for those who truly has no regard for the rules God has given us. Just remember that just as the days in the Bible presented obstacles to heaven's pathway, they still remain to this day. Just as the driver of sin that separates us from God, we must have a source greater than our own to overcome this great of a force (selfish desires coupled with the temptations of Satan).

Just as we consider the detrimental effects of this driver, we must look closely at God's means for recovery (redemption) back then and now. It must be noted that all forms of redemption God revealed to mankind, including the ultimate sacrifice Christ made for us, had to have one common denominator in order to redeem us—*faith*. The entire painting of the masterpiece has the color of faith prominently displayed. The painting is surrounded by a border of red, representing the blood of the one the painting amazingly displays. Yes, when all the color is added to this outline, a glorious and most beautiful portrait is made of the Son of God. He made it all possible. When you hear the old song "Reunited," think of the one in this painting as our means to be reunited with our Father.

Yet without faith, it is impossible to please God. Faith that moves us toward him and his provisions and nothing else. Did all those sacrifices made in Israel cleanse them for good? Absolutely not. Yet it did cover their sin until the next sacrifice was made. Therefore, their *faith* in what God said was the *means*, and it was their faith that God was seeking. God fully knew that no man could obey every law that he had given them. It would be some 1,400 years later that Israel's faith had to be placed on the one sacrifice for all our sin. This was completed by the shedding of blood of the Lamb of God, Jesus Christ. The Old Testament (Old Covenant) of the Bible looks forward to this great deliverance, and after his death, burial, and resurrection, we look back to this deliverance from sin.

While Israel never fully accepted Jesus as the Son of God nor his sacrifice that he made, there will be a day when they will. They will mourn when they see the scars and the wounds in his hands

(Zechariah 12:10). The book of Revelation seems to scare some and is left alone by many while searching the scriptures. However, one must understand the book deals with the final redemption of Israel and God making the final cleansing and judgment upon this earth. It rightly should scare those not prepared as there has never been a time on this planet when the wrath of God, the wrath of Satan, and the wrath of man all overwhelms the planet Earth. The Earth will tremble during this time yet will be fully restored just as God promised (Jeremiah 10:10). You like the looks and smell of that new car, wait and see what God does in the new earth! Now let's get back to the holiness of God.

As we look into the tabernacle, God instructed Moses very specifically on how to build it and how it was to be transported and approached. As Israel had very specific laws and procedures concerning this place of worship as well as *who* could enter in to the most holy place, the holy of holies. There could be an entire book written on this tabernacle, but we will briefly discuss its purpose and meaning as we journey on in the book of Leviticus. Several points should be made on this tabernacle of Moses as it was taken with them as a place of worship as they made their way to the Promised Land. Later a temple would be built by King Solomon in Jerusalem which would be destroyed by the Babylonians. The second temple would be reconstructed and later destroyed by the Romans in AD 70. The book of Revelation and Ezekiel reveals there will be another temple built in the latter days, and it is well known that all the plans have been made and preparations are in place to accomplish just that. There must be an event followed by a covenant made in Israel to allow this to happen (Daniel 9:27) as the temple site is currently under Muslim control. This is yet another development that confirms the truths of the Bible as everything is in place in Israel to rebuild the new temple and the pure-red heifer is now in Israel. The red heifer is essential for the ritual of purification and has to be an unblemished red heifer. After years of breeding, this enormous challenge has been met as another requirement for the third temple. Israel has made all the preparations needed to build the third temple as they are anxiously preparing for the Messiah to return.

The tabernacle of Moses, however, was a mobile type of tabernacle where Israel could worship and have atonement made for their sins. There was an outer court in which sacrifices were made by the priest, and only once a year did the priest enter the most holy place which was the inner court where God dwelled. A large curtain (veil) separated the two courts.

This day was set aside as the Day of Atonement or Yom Kippur. This is still the holiest day on the Jewish calendar. The only person permitted to enter the Holy of Holies was the high priest who had to be physically whole and from the ancestry of the tribe of Levi. Moses and his brother, Aaron, were from the tribe of Levi. The high priest would oversee the roles and responsibilities of the other priests. The high priest was the only one that could wear the Urim and the Thummim which were stones embedded in a vest the priest wore that would reveal the will of God. The high priest would have to make a sacrifice for his own sins first before making the sacrifice for the sins of Israel.

My friend, another book could be written on the depth of sin and all the sacrifices that were made from Adam and Eve until the arrival of *the* sacrifice, Jesus Christ. Man cannot erase the sin nor has any means to restore the cleansing that is required to restore being right with God (righteousness). "For all have sinned and come short of the glory of God" (Romans 3:23). The sacrificial ceremonies were only a temporary means to deal with the problem of sin and also pointed to one sacrifice that would be made for all our sin. However, one must have faith in "that while we were once sinners, Christ died for us." Again we must put our faith in his works as "it was his blood shed for the remission of sin."

Now we must consider, the high priest was the only one that could enter the temple and apply the blood to the altar. Anyone else that would enter this holy place would die on the spot. The high priest alone had to make a sacrifice for himself and then for the sins of Israel. During a sacrifice, the hand was placed on the head of the animal sacrificed as the sins of man were then transferred to the animal, and then it was killed and put on the altar to be completely burned up. This was nothing more than a shadow of our sin placed on the Son of God as he was killed and put on the cross (altar) for our sin. The blood is where the life is and the life was taken from the animal as well as the Son of God. Yet while the animal died, never to live again, the Lord Jesus arose from the dead, holding the keys of death and hell.

> **"I am he that liveth, and was dead, and behold, I am alive for evermore." Amen and have the keys of hell and of death.** (Revelation 1:18)

Many innocent animals died. Many animal's blood was shed. Many animals were laid on the altar to be burned completely up by the high priest.

Yet the process had to be completed over and over and over *until Jesus came*. It was the most important event in all of human history. Now, many souls would be saved. Now no more blood would have to be shed. Now, the veil of the temple was torn and no longer do we need a high priest to make sacrifices on our behalf. We may boldly have access to God through the finished work of his Son. Just as Israel's sins were too great and had to be transferred to an innocent animal, so are ours. Just as the entire animal had to be burned up to cover the sins, so now are the sins forever cleansed by our Lord, as His sacrifice was only needed once for the atonement of our sin. The burnt offering of the entire animal meant we would be entirely cleansed and that we look to the pure, innocent Son of God for our atonement.

It is interesting to note that the high priest, starting with the brother of Moses (Aaron), was of the tribe of Levi, yet Jesus came from the tribe of Judah. This difference signified that something better had to come, and that sacrificial lineage and roles fell short of the Levitical tribe and role. Something better—far better—was on its way and now all our sins have been burned up forever more. The high priest coming from the tribe of Levi provided a way temporarily to deal with our guilt problem, yet through the tribe of Judah would come the High Priest, the Son of God. I don't know how to describe such a sacrifice, such a gift, such mercy, such grace, and such love that can be attributed to God and to his Son. So as we complete the journey in Leviticus, let us forever remember just how holy and merciful God really is. While many laws, ceremonies, and sacrifices were made and established in this book, we must forever remember the major significance of this journey is this—God is Holy. God is worthy to be praised. We must be holy as God is Holy. We are made holy only through the atonement of sin through the pure innocent blood of the Son of God, Jesus Christ.

Don't mind all those critics making fun of you as being self-righteous and holier than thou as you strive to live a life following Christ. First and foremost, they are making fun of Christ first as you have claimed his sacrifice as your atonement, your holiness toward God. Secondly never mind them, as if their closet isn't full of trash if it would only be revealed by God. We shouldn't care as it is their day before God in judgment, they will give account for all of their words and works. Focus on the good things of people as everyone has baggage and wounds.

# Chapter 4

## A Journey in the Book of Numbers: Entry Denied

> **Thus Edom refused to give Israel passage through his border: wherefore Israel turned away from him. And the children of Israel, even the whole congregation, journeyed from Kadesh, and came unto mount Hor.**

You've planned your vacation of a lifetime as you have carefully saved and made reservations and are about to board the airplane, only to hear, "Your ticket is invalid, you cannot enter the aircraft." Disappointing, yes, to say the least. Yet the refusal-to-enter statement in this journey goes far beyond a dream vacation. In this journey, we will again visit the tribes of Israel as they were delivered out of bondage in Egypt and have been given rules, laws, and instructions on how to worship a holy God.

God had done something unique as to choose Moses to be his spokesperson to the new nation that God had chosen. Moses was the humblest person on earth at the time. This new nation of people was instructed on how to sanctify themselves through the purification and atonement of sin through sacrifice. Now direct communication was established by God himself, not only to Israel but to all of humanity and for all eternity. The newly blessed nation of people was the talk of the world as word spread of their God delivering them from a powerful Egyptian Army and world power.

These people are on their merry way to the Promised Land that God had promised their fathers Abraham, Isaac, and Jacob. Yet problems began to arise in the camp as a few bad apples began to complain, and it spread like a cancer within the tribes of Israel. The constant complaining and lack of faith during an eleven-day journey to the Promised Land would ultimately turn their "vacation" into a disaster. The eleven-day journey would turn into forty years wandering in the desert. Israel had sent twelve spies to explore the land of Canaan, and when they returned, all but Joshua and Caleb deemed themselves unfaithful to God. The majority of the spies convinced Israel that the walls were too fortified, and the vast armies of giants could not be defeated. A bad report, which ultimately disqualified all the adults of Israel to enter the Promised Land. It would only be the two faithful adult men who would enter into the land flowing with milk and honey. One must never minimize the foreshadowing of many events of the Bible to future events, both good and bad.

America must take heed of the fact that we must honor and obey God. He alone has parted the Red Sea for us and allowed our ancestors to enter a land flowing with milk and honey, just as the Pilgrims did. We saw that Israel had to fight for their land, just as we did. When the fighting ceased, Israel flourished just as the United States has. Many miracles were performed to form our country to where it is today. The same could be said for Israel as God miraculously fed them with manna (a bread, some call angels' food) and quail. Yet believe it or not, many complained and wished they were back in Egypt! The land of Egypt and her idols is a direct parallel to the lusts and idols of the world today. The constant complaining and the lack of faithfulness to God infuriated both God and Moses. Yet time after time, Moses would intercede for Israel and the mercy of God was granted over and over to this nation as they made their journey. There is perhaps no better time to explain the difference between the chastisement of God and the judgment of God. God chastises his children when they become disobedient. Jesus said, "I chasten those whom I love" as he was referring to his church, his followers.

Those that have rejected God are still under the curse of sin and are spiritually and eternally separated from God. This refusal of his love and his provisions ultimately means a fallen man without redemption falls into the judgment of a holy and just God. "It is a fearful thing to fall into the hands of the living God," and just as the scripture says, it will be devastating to all those facing the wrath and judgment of God. Yet he can never be blamed for making this judgment, as first of all, it is his right, being the Creator. He made the universe; he made us, and he makes the rules, period. His plan of redemption is the central and most valid message of the entire Bible. The Old Testament saints looked forward to the Savior as the New Testament Saints looked back to his finished work on the cross. Therefore, faith in Christ is the central message and theme for the entire Bible.

This is a simple message yet difficult to understand without going back into the Old Testament. Not having the background of the Old Testament is like eating a peanut butter sandwich without the jelly. We must reflect on the significance of the nation of Israel. There are so many lessons to be learned by careful study of both their history and their future. Again, just the mere fact of their existence today should prove the sovereignty and truthfulness of God. Critics will have their say, yet God will make a way, as He is the way, the truth and the life to those who follow him. Israel was chosen (sought out) by God, Israel was made a promise from God, Israel was subjected to great persecution, Israel was delivered by a savior from the bondage of Egypt and their own journey began to reach the promised land.

Likewise you were chosen by God, and his Word makes so many promises to you that it would take another book to even take a stab at it. Yet God promised us eternal life to those who merely accepts his plan of salvation and choose to follow Him. We too have a life to look forward to far beyond this one, where the milk and honey flows forever and ever. This promise will be fulfilled, and believe me, he can and will accomplish this. We too, as sinners in a fallen world, have the bondage of sin that encapsulates us all to different degrees. It rains on those in the family of God as well as those without. Sickness and disease fall upon those in the family as well as those without. Yet while we too suffer as believers in this fallen world, we have a secure promise that these sufferings of mountains and valleys are short-lived, and we have the blessed hope of eternal life; life with no suffering, no pain, and eternal peace and safety. We too have suffered persecution as believers as we have been ridiculed since the advent of Christ. We will continually be the minority until someday, we will be the only ones living on the new earth. Those refusing the hand of God and his righteousness will forever be living under the earth. The images of the unclothed Jews being slaughtered and covered up in large ravines in the earth will be replaced by those who pulled the triggers and ran over them with dozers being cast under the earth into the pits of hell forevermore. So it goes for the "final solution." We too were sent a Man of God, as in his Son who, like Moses, delivered a people out of bondage. It was Israel's mission to reflect God and eventually his Son who came unto his own (Jews) and they received him not. Yet some Jews did accept the Messiah and the early church was born. These fine called men of God (the apostles) were now completed Jews.

Never condemn the Jews if you don't want to be cursed. Most of the Jewish leaders and people denied Christ as they wanted a prince in shining armor to deliver them from the Roman Empire and rule the world. This again will happen but on God's time, not ours. The true "Anointed One" will return and will reign on earth forever. As most religions end human history with eternal peace on earth, there has been only one *Prince* on earth who could accomplish such a monumental task. This Prince was the only one who has healed the blind, raised the dead, and calmed the raging seas. His Father was the only one who could part the Red Sea and open the earth for evil folks to fall into the pits of hell (Numbers 16:32–33). There will be a future time when the antichrist will fool many as being the "anointed one," yet the wonders that he does are short-lived. Satan, just as in the days of Job, *will be given* power for forty-two months *by God* himself (Revelation 13:5). Beware if you are on earth during this time. The deceptive seeds of Satan will bloom only for a moment to be utterly destroyed by the stone the builders rejected, Jesus Christ.

Israel's journey still continues as they will understand in the near future that he *was and is* their Messiah. The very land where he was unmercifully beaten and crucified will be where he sets foot and sets his kingdom forever, in Jerusalem.

Now we can get a glimpse of why we should study the journeys of the Old Testament. We must ask the question while observing these twenty first and twenty second verses, who is denying Israel to pass through their borders? Why did they not allow them to pass through? This denial was devastating to them as now, their journey would take them through rough and unbearable terrain.

It isn't such a profound thought to know that God has enemies. It must also be assumed that those that follow him have the same common enemies. I assure you that if you take a true stand for God, the enemy will attack you, your family, and your livelihood. We see it in many places throughout the Bible, yet our journey here takes us to Edom, and the highway in their land makes it a quick and easy route to the Promised Land that Israel was travelling to. Yet all of Edom said, "No, you can't come through our land, or we will attack you with our huge army." Had these Edomites not heard of these people who were highly favored by God? You bet they did, yet these people were big time enemies of Israel. Their hatred for Israel goes all the way back to the patriarch Jacob and his brother Esau. The Edomites were descendants of Esau. God states in the Bible that "Esau I hate." The spirit of this wickedness goes from generation to generation, and we still see this evil spirit working against Israel to this very day.

So does God really hate Esau and those associated with him throughout the generations and even today? I refuse to put words in his mouth as I never would want to misrepresent or misquote God. Yet I feel it appropriate to say that God loves the person but hates his actions, and what he has stood for. Remember the person is a spirit and soul that just happens to live in this shell of a body. We must first acknowledge, honor, and serve him in spirit and in truth, not in the body. All other religions are actually working and feeding on emotion, feelings, and not in truth, which separates them from the

Spirit of God. It would be fair to say that while God loves the heart and soul of every person on earth, he despises the spirit of wickedness that not only is in high places over the earth but that which rests and dwells in the hearts of men. This spirit of wickedness keeps the soul separated from the spirit of God and rivals those living for him. It has blinded and deafened multitudes upon multitudes in the name of religion. The level and degree of this rivalry is both spiritual and physical,and is a direct affront to the Kingdom of God. It would be fair to say that the degree of rebellion and rejection of God varies from mild to extreme, yet all lead to death and destruction.

Why any person, any group of people, any king or kingdom would ever choose the spirit of wickedness over the most loving, the most caring and the most humble Spirit of God is beyond me. Yet a third of all the angelic beings in heaven chose this route, and it gets worse; most of humanity is led by this spirit of wickedness. We will learn through this journey to deny Israel is to deny the Most High God himself.

We will see throughout Esau's life that he would be rebellious to both his father and to God. Jacob and Esau were the twin sons of Isaac. When they were born, the younger son Jacob had his hand around his brother's ankle as they were born. They struggled not only coming out of the womb but also while they were in the womb. God told the mother, Rebecca, the older shall serve the younger as this created an eventual hatred between the brothers.

We must conclude that from birth, and even conception, this guy named Esau could be a bit rebellious and wild. He later in life became a great hunter, and one day, he came home starving while his brother Jacob had some soup that really looked and smelled delicious! Jacob offered his brother a bowl of soup for a little trade—Esau's birthright. It was a done deal for the hungry brother, and then later, Jacob tricked his ailing father into giving him the firstborn's blessings. Needless to say, this rivalry (while physical) could be labeled as spiritual as we recognize the trend of generational curses coupled with spiritual influences from Esau's descendants. The jealousy and resentment that Esau had for Jacob was only fueled even more when Esau intermarried with Ishmael's daughter. Ishmael was later credited for the religion of Islam as he was a child of Abraham's maid, Hagar. Abraham, Isaac, and Jacob were not all perfect folks, but they all had one thing in common—they were faithful and dedicated to God.

While Esau shared in God's blessings, we must look beyond his relationship to the Patriarchs and consider the deep rooted rivalry that exists to this day. This rivalry remains as the disputed land issue fuels their hatred toward Israel. As we are clearly living in the last days, we see this rivalry heating up more and more. It must also be mentioned that some have converted from these false religions. It must be made clear that God loves the Muslim, the fighters for ISIS and Hezbollah, and all the descendants of both Ishmael and Esau. It is my prayer that these people will more and more see the light of truth and follow it while it is available to them. The narrow road to heaven may be taken by anyone, regardless of the current religion or situation they may be in. It is a difficult decision, yet a wise one to turn away from the worldly pathway of pressures and pleasures that most of humanity are treacherously taking.

Future journeys will further discuss this spiritual and generational conflict that exists with the nation of Israel.

So as we currently witness the conflict in the Middle East, we need to look no further than the days of Esau and Jacob when it all began. The Edomites refused to allow Israel to pass through land that will ultimately become Israel's land as promised by God in Genesis chapter 15. We still witness the ancestors of Esau continuing this rivalry as we read the world news today. Their goal is to wipe the Jew off the map, the same goal that was promoted by Pharaoh, Haman, King Herod, Hitler and the soon coming Antichrist. Their goal was and will be defeated by the Word of God.

Now let's go to our next journey in the book of Deuteronomy.

# Chapter 5

## A Journey in the Book of Deuteronomy: Innocent from Murder

> **If one be found slain in the land which the LORD thy God giveth thee to possess it, lying in the field, and it be not known who hath slain him. Then thy elders and thy judges shall come forth, and they shall measure unto the cities which are round about him that is slain.**

In Israel's journey, it was apparent that there were occurrences when someone found a dead person along the way. As the twenty-first and twenty-second verses following chapter 20 go into the next chapter, we address the seriousness of mankind shedding innocent blood. Blood is the lifeline to both man and beast, and without it, no life would exist. We have already visited the means for man to be forgiven of sin by the sacrifice of an innocent animal after the sins have been transferred from the man to the animal. Then blood is shed as the animal dies. As the animal dies, so does the sin that was applied to the animal.

It is amazing, however, to visit a story of a murder and of innocent blood when the son of Adam, Cain, killed his brother, Abel. Just as we previously discussed how Esau was jealous of his brother Jacob, Cain, likewise, was jealous of Abel. They both had made offerings to God, and Cain chose to make an offering that was not suitable to God but for him. When God accepted his brother's offering and rejected his, Cain became furious and killed his brother. The story goes that God approached Cain, and the question arises of his brother's fate.

> **And he said, what hast thou done? The voice of thy brother's blood crieth unto me from the ground. And now art thou cursed from the earth, which hath opened her mouth to receive thy brother's blood from thy hand.** (Genesis 4:10)

We have already discussed the complexities and perfection of the functions of the human body, and we should all marvel at such a creation. We haven't the time to debate the interpretation of true scientific data on our design nor the dating of the elements. Blood, again, makes life possible in the human body. The body is an amazing creation when put under a microscope. The mere complexity of the cellular structure of DNA is proof in itself that coincidence is not acceptable to most reasoning when considering the design of the human body. The delicate design of the human body is nothing short of remarkable. As we consider the vastness of the universe, we should also marvel at the perfect atmosphere God created for us to dwell in. Such a waste of time and energy is made for denying the truth of our origin. Wisdom begins only by fearing God and his Word of truth. Science will prove design if you look deep enough into it. Too many highly educated folks foolishly question the Creator which is not only unwise, but they are requiring pure logic and reasoning to be forfeited to prove their interpretation of certain scientific evidence. Don't be one of the arrogant that God laughs at in Psalm 2. Education without sanctification is an abomination. It is impossible to be sanctified outside of God's provisions.

There once was a mother and child visiting the zoo when the mother lost control of the baby carriage, and it rolled down the hill to the monkey cage. The mother had just given her child a banana to feed the monkeys, as she lost control of the stroller. It happened quickly, and the carriage rammed into the monkey cage. The monkey, seeing the carriage coming down the hill, showed no emotion as she saw the defenseless child barreling toward her. The panic and scream of the mother also provided no response from the monkey. But other humans rushed to try to stop the child. Yet when the stroller hit the cage, the monkey reacted as she was startled and jumped back momentarily.

The young child was thrown out of the stroller and somehow was still holding onto the banana. The monkey raced to the child and snatched the banana from the child's hand. Most evolutionists would agree that *similar* DNA was present here—the monkey *reacted* to the accident, and the monkey ate just as we do. While other monkeys raced to get a possible bite of banana, other *humans* raced to aid the child. *The tears* of fear shed by the mother were turned to tears of joy when she saw that her child was okay. She thanked all those who came to comfort her and the child.

The truth is that God created you and the monkey, and He gave them both abilities. While those abilities may have adapted and evolved, a monkey is still a monkey some six thousand years later. The monkey had the ability to carry her child on her back, and she did it well and has for over six thousand years. Man was given the ability to take elements and make fabrics and plastics and metals, then a stroller. Both had the ability to react as the monkey ran away from the child, yet those with emotion and reasoning ran toward the child. Both had the ability for appreciation as the monkeys all raced to the cage rails to grab the last banana while the mother hugged those that aided her and her child. Evolutionists may convince some of their colleagues of their theory, but they would never convince this mother!

There is no monkeying around when it comes to shedding the blood of God's creation as we look back in the fourth chapter of Genesis. This is where Adam's son Cain slew his brother Abel. We see the unseen world here for a moment as God tells Cain that his brother's blood is crying out to him from the earth. Just as judgment was placed on Cain, as he was cursed from that day until his death, man will be accountable for shedding innocent blood as well. God had commanded Israel not to murder when he gave them the Ten Commandments. There were apparently times that a murder scene was encountered as Israel was travelling, and God made a provision for them so they would not be held accountable for the blood and the life that was taken. They had a procedure they had to follow that proved their innocence. The blood of man is pure and powerful, as it represents life both in man and animal. If a sparrow loses its life, God knows. If a man or woman loses their lives, God knows it. If a child loses their life, God knows it, whether it is in the womb or not, God hears the cry of the child. While blood is on the hands of many in this world, it can be quickly washed away by the blood of the Lamb for those who trust in him. You just have to ask him, and you will be forgiven.

You ask anyone who has performed an abortion, and they would be lying if they said there was no blood involved in the taking of a life. In China alone, there will be approximately ten million children killed by the Chinese government this year alone. New York has boasted of an abortion bill that Governor Cuomo signed into law that allows abortion regardless of what the US Supreme Court rules. The latest statistics places New York at having one of the highest abortion rates in the US. This is not a statistic to be proud of.

The tribes of Israel, on the same note, were commanded not to sacrifice their children to the false god Molech (Deuteronomy 12:31). The shedding of innocent blood is a great offense to both the child and the Almighty God. The Canaanites worshipped a false god, Molech, which required placing a child (usually the firstborn) in the arms of the idol Molech and burned to death. Multitudes of innocent children were sacrificed and their lives taken for the sake of a stone rock idol. In China, multitudes of men face a life without a bride because their government killed most of the girls. While that is not near the end of the significance of this great sin, it does present only a part of the result of this sin.

God is telling Israel in this journey that innocent blood is of great importance to him and should be to all who are breathing upon this earth. Also he is telling them a way not to be liable for the shedding of innocent blood. Another point to be made here is that an offence was made by someone to have murdered this person that was found. Yet an innocent life had to be taken (a sacrifice of an animal) for everyone in Israel to be cleared of this murder. This could again be another reference that we are all living in a world of sin; while there is one who is accountable (Adam), we all must deal with the consequences and that is the judgment of God. The subject of blood will continue throughout these journeys as we get a grip on just how powerful and how pure the blood of Christ actually is. It's power frees us from all the corruption in our own lives and rids the influence of our past generations as some have been cursed. The shed blood of Christ was a game changer for all life, death, and hell. The necessity for such atonement proves more and more critical as we continue our journey in 2022. We will go twenty two verses from chapter 20, now in the book of Joshua to cross the Jordan River into the land of Canaan. Canaan is the land God promised Israel.

# CHAPTER 6

## A Journey in the Book of Joshua: An Early Reward

**But the field of the city, and the villages thereof, gave they to Caleb the son of Jephunneh for his possession. Thus they gave to the children of Arron the priest Hebron with her suburbs, to be a city of refuge for the slayer, and Libnah with her suburbs.**

It seems that Joshua gets a lot of attention (and for good reason) after Moses dies and is buried by God. Joshua took the leadership role that God gave him, and he took the next generation of Israelites across the Jordan river into the land of Canaan. It is amazing to see God part the Red Sea to get them out of bondage and then part the Jordan River (probably at flood stage) to get them in to the Promised Land. Canaan was a beautiful land yet filled with ungodliness and idolatry. The land was theirs, but many battles had to be won that would fulfill God's promise and bring glory to his kingdom. Canaan's idol worship represented the darkened sea of the world as they denied the true God of heaven.

> **And the light of Israel shall be for a fire, and his Holy One for a flame. and it shall burn and devour his thorns and his briers in one day.** (Isaiah 10:17)

**A light to lighten the Gentiles, and the glory of thy people Israel.** (Luke 2:32)

The light most certainly did lighten the Gentiles as we read in Paul's letter to the Ephesians,

**"Now unto him that is able to do exceeding abundantly above all that we ask or think, according to the power that worketh in us. Unto him be glory in the church by Christ Jesus throughout all the ages, world without end, Amen"** (Ephesians 3:20–21).

Just as the Promised Land would now be taken by Joshua, Caleb, and the nation of Israel, so will the earth be taken back to the kingdom of God throughout the ages in a world with no end. Remember, it is *His* earth. It is not only our prayer that "thy kingdom come, thy will be done, on earth as it is in heaven," it will be a reality and a promise kept by God. This earth will be cleansed of all evil, and God promises "the meek shall inherit the earth," and Jerusalem will be God's dwelling place forever. There is some healthy debate as to our final resting place being here (current earth that is cleansed) or on an entirely new planet. It is fun to debate and share our thoughts on secondary issues within the faithful of God. I personally think we will be here, on a totally sin free world, when all the smoke and fire clears.

So the light of the world now comes within those hearts and souls of the church and shines to an even larger land than Egypt or Canaan. The truth of God must be communicated from one end of the earth to the other. The truth of God leaves no debate as it clearly states the will of God and the way of salvation to all of humanity. It also clearly declares the destiny of every soul as one destined to the wrath and judgment of God or to the abundant grace and mercy given to those who diligently seek Him with their hearts:

> **And ye shall seek Me, and find Me, when ye shall search for Me with all your heart"** (Jeremiah 29:13).

You see, there are too many souls out there whose words have claimed to be Christians, yet their prayers never make it to heaven. They never make it because their heart is far from the Father. The deep intention of their heart is to please oneself and not to please the Creator of all things. Their words speak glory and praise to God, but they are words only, with no deep regard to please and know the one and only true God. He is not there for those who merely call on His name once in a while. He is only there for those who seek Him with all their heart. There is nothing more needed in the world today than the truth of God given to those searching for it. Remember by purchasing this book, you have honored God by placing his word throughout the world and being a part of fulfilling this scripture:

> **And the Gospel must first be published among all the nations.** (Mark 13:10)

As Joshua was remembered as one of God's faithful servants, we should strive as well to spread the good news promised by God.

We are now getting a better understanding of God's plan as we follow these people into the land of Canaan. God sought a people to be his own (family). God found them. God taught them provisions of his law to be counted worthy to be reunited with him (shedding of blood through sacrifices). God made a promise to them (a land for everlasting possession) for their faithfulness. It is his plan that they be his people, and he will be their God and our God as he resides in Jerusalem. That day will come.

As Christians, we realize we have been adopted into God's family and are beneficiaries of the promises of our Father. Careful study will reveal that both Israel and the church have been made separate promises, yet there are many promises made that include both the church and Israel. Always remember, church, that we are the adopted ones! Never forget your roots. We need to pray for peace in Jerusalem. He will come back someday soon, and they will accept the Prince of Peace. He will secure their final and eternal resting place and deliverance. This final redemption of Israel will be complete as we complete our final journey in the book of Revelation.

As we examine the twenty-first and twenty-second verses in chapter 20 (these verses go into the next chapter), we begin to see the promise of reward from God begin to take place with Caleb. If you recall, only two of the spies sent to the Promised Land returned to Israel with a good report. Only Caleb and Joshua had the faith that they could win the battles and take the land which God had promised them.

> **And Caleb stilled the people before Moses, and said, "Let us go up at once, and possess it; for we are well able to overcome it."** (Numbers 13:30)

The other ten spies had the spirit of fear and unbelief and had convinced Israel that the cities were too fortified, and the armies of giants were too intimidating to mess with. Oh, would this chosen people of God forfeit this land of milk and honey to go back into bondage in the land of Egypt? Unfortunately most of them would have! It not only takes an act of faith to be on God's side, but it takes work and action to support such faith. We see early on that this man, Caleb, was on fire for the *Lord*. He said, "We are able because the *Lord* is able." Caleb just didn't think their Savior delivered them by a fire by night and a cloud by day from Pharaoh's advancing army. *He was moved by it.* Caleb just didn't see the sea parting to pave their way to the Promised Land, *he was moved by it.* Caleb just didn't hear the Creator of heaven and earth, *he was moved by his voice.* Caleb saw the glory and the miracles of the Lord, and it moved *his soul and spirit into action and deed.* Caleb's actions were a direct result of his unwavering faith in God.

Yet we see the majority of the camp were persuaded by the other ten spies as they were merely grasshoppers against giants, and despite all the glory and miracles shown to them by God, they weren't moved in their hearts. Fear overtook them. Faith in these ten spies' report cost them forty years of wandering in the wilderness only to die. Every day (forty) the unfaithful spies searched out the Promised Land would be rewarded a year wandering in the desert. They would never enter into the Promised Land.

> **Because all those men which have seen my glory, and my miracles, which I did in Egypt and in the wilderness, and have tempted me now these ten times, and have not hearkened to my voice; Surely they shall not see the land which I sware unto their fathers, neither shall any of them that provoked me see it: But my servant Caleb, because he had another spirit with him, and hath followed me fully, him will I bring into the land whereinto he went; and his seed shall possess it.** (Numbers 14:22–24)

It should be noted here two things that God points out to Moses when stating the sentence to Israel for their unbelief: he addresses and recognizes the spirit Caleb had as well as the intentions of his heart. The words "followed me fully" are just a few words, but it reveals volumes, my friend. Yes, there were giants in the land to be taken; yes, their armies were huge, and the walls of the cities were heavily fortified. But Caleb never hesitated in believing the victory was theirs with the Lord on their side. One should never underestimate the joy, peace, and confidence one has when being faithful to God. Caleb and Joshua had their reward coming, as well as the children of Israel. The adults of Israel were rewarded with forty years of wandering in the desert until the adults died. It was only their children, Caleb, and Joshua who would see the Promised Land. All those living in Israel at the age of twenty and above died in the wilderness.

Just as our journeys in this book echoes many of the same themes, we will see a similar pattern of rewards, both good and bad. Many people are seen as being moved by the right spirit as well as some moved by the wrong spirit.

It should be noted here and beyond that the majority chose the wrong spirit as we read on. The majority of the spies (ten of them) convinced the entire camp that God was not able to deliver them. This spirit of fear and unbelief disappointed and infuriated God and for good reason. We must all seriously evaluate our position with God as to our actions in spirit and in body. Just as you choose the food you eat, you also choose the food you fill your mind with. One sad fact that truly disappoints God is the time and energy his children put in to objects in their hand (phones and gaming controls) and what little time they spend on studying his Word. Are we fully following him and worshiping him in Spirit and in truth?

We, like Israel, have our instructions from God (his Holy Word), and we have the land to conquer, (evil of this world) to shed his light (truth, peace, and joy) to the darkened world of sin. Yet after one becomes a true believer, he must strive to be a faithful believer and to keep a conquering spirit in all situations. We do not work for the victory, but we work *through* the victory. The victory was won by faith in the finished work of Jesus Christ. That alone will sustain us and equip us for the spiritual battlefield the family of God faces in this world today (Ephesians 6). Caleb's faith in the Word of God was unwavering, and we should follow Caleb's example.

Faithfulness of one can also affect the generations to follow as God not only promises Caleb a reward, but the reward also is enjoyed by his children.

> **Save Caleb the son of Jephunneh; he shall see it, and to him will I give the land that he hath trodden upon, and to his children, because he hath wholly followed the Lord.**
> (Deuteronomy 1:36)

The place in time we go to in this journey takes place where a faithfully dedicated person who wholly followed the Lord is rewarded. The rewards in this journey were to both the children of Arron the priest and to Caleb as we see God remembers those who honor Him. It again is a pattern we see throughout the Bible to many faithful men and women. It is my prayer that you place yourself in that number of the called, the chosen, and the *faithful*. If you were to die at this very moment, what would be your reward when you meet God?

Perhaps one of the best messages that comes from the book of Joshua is this one:

> **And I have given you a land for which ye did not labour, and cities which ye built not, and ye dwell in them; of the vineyards and oliveyards which ye planted not do ye eat. Now therefore fear the LORD, and serve him in sincerity and in truth: and put away the gods which your fathers served on the other side of the flood, and in Egypt; and serve ye the LORD. And it seem evil unto you to serve the LORD, choose you this day whom ye will serve; whether the gods which your fathers served that were on the other side of the flood, other gods of the Amorites, in whose land ye dwell; but as for me and my house, we will serve the LORD.** (Joshua 24:13–15)

As we carefully read this scripture, we must truly humble ourselves as we consider our new and perfect bodies that we will be given were not conceived by us but by the hand of God. That our beautiful new earth we will enjoy was made for us and we had no ability to contribute to such a gift. That we have our own eternal dwelling made not by our own hammer and nails but by a nail-scarred hand that we hung on a cross. Get on your knees and thank God, thank Jesus, and thank the Holy Spirit for all the thought, all the love, all the work, and all the sacrifice that was made for such gifts that await us!

This journey was one of victory and not only tells of God rewarding the faithfulness of an individual, but why he did. Caleb and Joshua went against all odds as the other ten spies conspired to convince all of Israel that the land could not be taken. The words *fully* and *wholly* explain the why Caleb was rewarded. There is diversity in the family of God, in that there are those that contribute little to the kingdom of God and those that sacrifice daily and give their all. Examine your life and choose ye this day who you will serve, and oh, yes, my friend, serve Him fully and wholly while you have the breath to do so.

Our next journey is no longer victorious, as we see the reverence and obedience Israel had for God begins to waiver after Joshua and Caleb had died.

# Chapter 7

## A Journey in the Book of Judges: Civil War

**And the children of Benjamin came forth out of Gibeah, and destroyed down to the ground of the Israelites that day twenty and two thousand men. And the people, the men of Israel, encouraged themselves and set their battle again in array in the place where they put themselves in array the first day.**

Are you kidding me? Aren't these folks of Benjamin part of the twelve tribes of Israel? Wasn't Benjamin Jacob's youngest son? Then how on earth could these guys kill twenty-two thousand of their brothers in a single day? Well, fast-forward around three thousand years, and you will find a strikingly similar number of soldiers killed right here on American soil. The Second Battle of Bull Run was a horrible sight to see of all the beloved sons of both the North and the South, lying all over the battlefield. The same could be said of the civil war taking place in Israel.

What in the world could cause these good God-fearing people to go out and kill over twenty thousand souls in a single day? In the States, some folks needed slaves to help out for their business and work at the homeplace, while others here in America, including Abraham Lincoln, knew it was wrong. When all the smoke cleared, there were over six hundred thousand Americans killed. There is one common factor in both civil wars and it was this: division, explosion, and then climax. It is well known, the division that existed back in 1860 between the North and the South. This division grew and gained enough steam that the explosion (acts and battles) climaxed with over six hundred thousand sons and fathers killed. The two battles of Bull Run gave the South victories against all odds and gave them a false sense of strength that eventually crumbled. There are horrifying photographs of the Civil War showing bodies piled and lying everywhere.

We, as Americans can relate to this carnage as we well know our history, and while it was part of our history, we wished it never happened, as so many lives were lost. War is bad enough as we must all unite against the apparent and ulterior motives of evil. The American Civil War took quite a while to get into direct conflict, yet this war in Israel happened so quickly, we must ask ourselves, who was in charge here? It was definitely not Abraham Lincoln, but if you carefully read the book of Judges, you will see there was no king in Israel. They all did what was right in their eyes, not the eyes of God. This is a recipe for destruction for any soul, group, or society. This is a recipe for disaster. In both civil wars, we see the division, then the explosion that was ignited by a deep belief opposite of the other side's opinion that was worth fighting and dying for.

When considering the slavery during the 1800s, we know it was morally wrong. Yet, due to the need for labor for personal and business needs, some folks here were morally wrong to condone slavery for just a benefit. There is no respecter of persons in the eyes of God, and we should treat all human beings at the same level. It was Adolph Hitler that convinced many that they were a superior race, and he acted as a god to discern things he had no right nor authority to determine. It is alarming, however, just how a person's stand, whether right or wrong, can be followed by such a multitude so quickly yet so blindly. This one man's evil belief was attractive to a few, then to more and more, and as the explosions could be heard on the beaches of Normandy, so were the minds of those fighting ferociously for the Axis powers. They were brainwashed, fighting for a lost cause and a loser for a leader. The climax came as both Germany and Japan surrendered, but not until some seventy-five million people were killed.

War and the spirit of war goes back to the first civil war described in Genesis as Adam's son Cain killed his brother Abel, as we discussed in an earlier journey. It is hard enough to consider war and its atrocities, but it is really disturbing when brothers are killing brothers. We see history repeating itself in so many ways as we look at the short six thousand years we have been living on this planet. It seems we never learn, but I can assure you that there is one final war in the last book of the Bible that will be the last one. The source that waters that seed and nurtures it will be forever defeated. War on earth and the desire for war will no longer exist. While we are living in the last days, we hear of rumors of war, and the world has never been prepared for war like it is now.

We see Russia and China flexing their muscle as they have dramatically built a large military presence in arms and personnel. China is a supporter of the enemies of Israel, and Russia is a staunch supporter of Iran. Iran screams every single day, "Death to America, and death to Israel." As we have discussed the uprising of evil in this world, there is perhaps no better example than that of Russia's aggression throughout Europe as well as the rumors of China planning their own aggressions. The war described in Revelation where one-third of mankind is killed could easily happen through a nuclear conflict.

We now see a major nuclear power threatening the use of such weapons, and while we are not currently in the tribulation, it is yet another sign that we are living in the last days. Again, Jesus said when these things ***begin*** to come to pass, look up and lift your heads, for your redemption draweth nigh (Luke 21:28). Now let's return to this journey in Israel as another war is about to erupt.

Again remember the main theme in this entire book of Judges is that Israel had no king, no leader, and no direction as man did what was right in his own eyes. We are about to see just what happens when there is no leader to a nation. There was a man from the tribe of Levi that had a concubine that had been unfaithful to him, and she left him. She went to her father's home in Bethlehem for four months. The Levite then travelled to Bethlehem to visit her and her father, hoping she would return to him.

It is interesting to note that the father-in-law seemed pleased from the start to see the Levite as he encouraged him to stay with them day after day. He stayed there for four nights, and on the fifth day, the Levite was invited once again to spend the night by the girl's father, but he insisted on leaving despite it getting very late in the evening. The Levite and his servant packed everything on the donkeys, and the three of them left late in the evening. While passing the city of Jebus (Jerusalem), the servant asked the Levite to stop there to spend the night; however, the Levite refused. His reasoning was that they would pass the city of the Jebusites (a tribe of the Canaanites) to a safer location where fellow Israelites dwelled. So, they journeyed on to the city of Gibeah. This city was in the territory of the tribe of Benjamin, and the Levite felt it was a safe place to spend the night as their fellow tribesmen would take care of them.

They apparently stayed in the streets there for quite some time until an old farmer passed by, who had been working in the fields all day. It is interesting to note that the farmer said, "Peace be with thee," and invited them to his home to spend the night. The farmer took them in, fed their donkeys, and prepared dinner for them. All seemed to be going well, and I'm sure the Levite had thought he had made a good decision to leave late, to pass an unfriendly city, and now to stay in a city where "peace would be with him." Yet things began to go horribly wrong when some men of the city started beating on the door. These men had gathered from the city and came with intentions to have sexual relations with the Levite. It is sad to see the response of the farmer as he offered the men his own daughter in the place of the Levite in order to protect his guest. The men refused the farmer's request, and then the story gets even worse as the Levite puts his concubine out for the men to have. The men then proceed to abuse her throughout the night and early the next morning she comes to the doorstep and dies. One could hardly imagine the pain and anguish this poor woman endured. The Levite and his servant then took the woman and put her on her donkey and went home. After arriving at home, the Levite then cuts the woman into twelve parts and sends them to the twelve tribes of Israel. Now the seeds of war have been planted.

One must consider that nothing of this sort had ever happened in the tribes of Israel, as they quickly wanted to know how and why such a thing happened. The tribes of Israel assembled, and the Levite addressed them and told his story to the assembly. There was little debate as Israel was infuriated at such an atrocity, and they quickly assembled an army to make justice for this evil act that had been done. There was a brief bit of diplomacy done as many went into the tribe of Benjamin seeking the men that were responsible for the evil act, yet here is where the division comes to the surface. They refused Israel's request and chose to defend their own, even if it was wrong.

This situation should have never existed as the men of Gibeah should have been at home, sleeping that night instead of being the worthless and evil men that they were. The Levite and the farmer could have fought the men, and perhaps the girl could have fled to safety during the fight. Yet the Levite could have heeded the wise advice from the girl's father and stayed home, as it was really too late to be making such a long journey home. Yet, hindsight is always twenty-twenty, and now bad decisions led to even worse decisions on both sides, and now the explosion is about to begin.

As the scripture in Judges 20:21–22 reveals, the army of Benjamin came out of the city of Gibeah and killed twenty-two thousand of the tribe of Judah. This was devastating to Israel as they assembled and sought the *Lord*, only to be told to go on and fight again. The second battle was again devastating as eighteen thousand more from Israel were slain. In both cases of this war, as well as the American Civil War, the early victory of the wrong side gained confidence, yet it was a false sense of hope. Just as the South's early victories gave them a false sense of hope, so it was for the tribe of Benjamin and their army. Both had won two battles decisively, yet they would ultimately lose the war. Defending a gang of rapists. Defending rights to own what is not theirs to own (slavery). Both beliefs were terribly wrong, yet while the close relationship of both parties were present (even being in the same tribe, same family, same country, same fellowship), these beliefs overruled all logic and was morally wrong. There were good people in the South and the tribe of Benjamin, yet division in beliefs escalated tragically in both wars.

One's belief system begins at an early age as parents are first responsible for raising their children to respect the rights of others, the needs of others, and the care of others. In these civil wars, we can see a lot of folks not heeding this mutual respect for other human beings. Every human being has a God-given sense of right and wrong. A rival to this God-given nature is pure selfish motives that dominate a person or a group of persons. Satan is a master of feeding the spiritually weak-minded the poison that overrules the good nature given by God. That nature, however, can be manipulated and controlled by the evil forces of this world and those advancing it.

As earlier mentioned, war has been with us since the days of Cain and Abel, back in the earliest days of human history. As we look around us in Ukraine, Syria and Yemen, we can see war is still with humanity. Just as in these two cases mentioned, we must conclude to all of those considering fighting for the wrong side. The tribe of Benjamin, the South, and even Adolph Hitler all had early victories and false hope spread throughout all their camps early. Yet Cain was cursed by God, the tribe of Benjamin was utterly destroyed, slavery was defeated by the North in the United States, and Hitler and all his army was defeated. Millions upon millions died throughout the ages because of trying to make wrongs right, and this belief, while detrimental to the multitudes, will exist until the final war described in Revelation.

While those supporting the wrong side and a wrong motive previously mentioned are long dead and gone, the spirit of division is alive and well on planet Earth. These spirits never rest as they have been controlling the minds of parents, politicians, kings, teachers, professors, presidents, religious cults, and all false religions, even to this day. The seeds are planted, and remember, the seeds begin to sprout in division in the mind and soul. The spiritual warfare that goes on may be invisible at its source, but its effect is obvious as we see yet today. The cities are burning in division and chaos. Peaceful protesting is healthy as the voices of all humanity have a right to be expressed. If everyone would just live the life of obeying the first and second commandments Jesus spoke of, there would be no need for protesting. Yet, evil motives creep into these reasonable and peaceful protests and turn violent. We should pray for not only peace in Jerusalem but peace in our cities as well. There is a war to silence those not of this world and stand for the truths of God. It is becoming evident and even prophesied how those representing the Kingdom of God will become more and more offensive to this world (1 Peter 2:8–9). The kingdom of God is certainly not welcomed in the world today. The war against those truly on God's side is raging and is being expressed more and more as the last days are rapidly approaching mankind. The radical and rivalry spirit of rebellion toward the kingdom of God will meet its end as prophesied in both the New and the Old Testaments. At that point in time, Satan gathers his forces and those who choose to follow him one final time to battle, and God utterly destroys them all. **"And the devil that deceived them was cast into the lake of fire and brimstone, where the beast and the false prophet are, and shall be tormented day and night for ever and ever"** (Revelation 20:10).

During all wars, there are motives on each side, and through the thousands of wars fought upon this earth, there were good people fighting for the wrong cause which ultimately ruined their families, their home, and their dreams. One can blame the forces of evil that deceived these good men and women who fought for the wrong cause, but ultimately, it was their own responsibility. If you have not raised your children in the right way, then you have failed. But the good news is that you can still make up for lost time and reconcile with your children and tell them you were wrong in not bringing them up by honoring and serving the *Lord* of hosts. Give them a copy of this book and a copy of the Bible. There is no better gift to give your children but that of peace. Peace of mind. Peace of security. Peace of God.

Remember, the farmer had told the Levite, "Peace be with you," as they were comforted with his hospitality. Yet evil came upon them that night and spread its venom that caused a war among the tribes of Israel. After Jesus Christ was ridiculed, forsaken, beaten, and crucified on the cross, he arose the third day and appeared to his disciples. As he appeared to them in the upper room, his first words to his disciples should be the last words you hear each night as you go to sleep; Jesus said, "Peace be unto you."

Place your trust in the Prince of Peace and rest in Him through all of eternity.

There will be war no more.

# CHAPTER 8

# A Journey in 1 Samuel: A True Friend

**And behold, I will send a lad, saying, Go, find out the arrows are on this side of thee, take them; then come thou; for there is peace to thee, and no hurt; as the L**ORD** liveth. But if I say thus unto the young man, Behold the arrows are beyond thee; go thy way: for the L**ORD** hath sent thee away.**

There is nothing better than a good true friend. The Bible is full of men and women who you would love having as your friend, yet many that you would prefer not to. This message goes right into the middle of a great friendship back in the early days of King David. David was not king at this moment in time, but it was King Saul who was the father of David's best friend, Jonathan. King Saul was extremely jealous of David and, as we discover in this journey, seeks the life of David. Yet, Jonathan proves his friendship is genuine and unwavering as he warns David of his father's evil intentions.

So why would the king of Israel be jealous over an unknown son of Jesse? I guess we should first discuss how we went from Israel being led by Moses, then through Judges, and now to Kings as we bring to the table, kings of Israel. The journey of Israel never ended after the Romans leveled the temple in AD 70. Many have different views on their role then and now, and it is really not that difficult when you study the Old Testament. During the Roman time, Israel was looking for the Messiah (King) to come, and when he did, he was not the magnificent king coming to establish his Kingdom in Jerusalem. They were not looking for a babe wrapped in swaddling clothes, nor did they want a king who would enter the eastern gate on a donkey as Jesus did. So remember they are still looking for the Messiah and the Anointed One. As we discussed earlier, we will take the journey when the King of kings does come in great power and great glory to reclaim the earth and to establish his everlasting kingdom on earth.

Joshua and Caleb began the journey, as previously discussed, by God miraculously parting the swollen Jordan River when she was raging at flood stage. The priests were instructed to take the ark of the covenant and to go into the midst of the river. As soon as their feet touched the water, it parted, and they carried the ark to the middle of the riverbed. All the tribes who stood far off saw the river parting and then began their journey to conquer the Promised Land. It wasn't until all three million of them passed the ark did the Levites begin to move the ark in following behind those as they travelled to dry ground. It was God's way of telling his people to leave no doubt, that he would provide a way for them to the Promised Land and that he would always be behind them. After the land was conquered, the land was divided among the twelve tribes. Through all their ups and downs in serving God, twelve judges were sent to provide leadership for the tribes. They had to settle disputes and administer justice, which was an uphill battle during the time of Israel when they had no king. It was a time of mostly failure as disobedience prevailed most of the time, and Israel suffered immensely. Joshua was the first judge, and Samuel was their last judge before Israel had their first king, King Saul.

While this story visits a close friendship with David, we begin also to see the development of a chosen King for Israel. A king that would lead a nation chosen by the God of Abraham, Isaac, and Jacob. This nation would be blessed, yet these journeys have proven that when they stray, God chastises them. We see the priests enter the scene and their need. We see the judges on the scene as they have to provide leadership to attempt to keep peace and order during their stay in the Promised Land. The leadership role from judges to kings comes into focus in this journey as we are right in the middle of a king who disobeyed God. God has utterly rejected King Saul for not doing what God had instructed, and the Spirit of God left this king. Israel requested a king, and God had determined that David, the son of Jesse, would be the man (a very young man).

King Saul had a troubling spirit that could only be calmed when David would play the harp for him. Saul would call for him often as he was tormented by this troubling spirit. The friendship begins as Saul's son, Jonathan, and David meet, and David finds a friend who eventually saves his life. God had told the last judge, Samuel, to go the family of Jesse, and he would find the new king he wanted to rule Israel. Samuel was introduced to all the sons but the shepherd boy in the hills tending the sheep. None of the sons were the called ones, and Samuel asked Jesse, "Are these all of your sons?" Jesse responded that the youngest son was tending the sheep. David was called to them, and as soon as Samuel saw David, God said that he was the one chosen to be king. That son of Jesse later made a name for himself as the Philistines (powerful enemy of Israel) had a commander named Goliath (who was extremely tall and enormous in size) who would meet David on the battlefield.

King Saul and Israel were terrified of this warrior and his vast army of soldiers. Goliath and his army would come out each morning from their camp, and he would challenge Israel each morning to send a warrior to fight him. He defied Israel for forty days, and David's oldest brothers were at the battlefield during this time. David was sent by his father to take food to his brothers, and the eldest was jealous of David and made fun of him. Yet David pursued the matter and was greatly offended as the giant of the Philistines defied the army of "the living God," as David quoted. King Saul called for David, and he explained that he would go fight the giant. David was more than qualified as he had killed a lion and a bear with his hands that were attacking his father's sheep.

The king put his armor on David to prepare the youth for the fight, but David humbly took it off, saying he was not worthy to wear such armor. Here we see the failure of the presiding king and the early signs of a new king whom God had chosen. David went to the battlefield and confronted Goliath, and he made fun of David, which was his second mistake. To make fun of God's chosen is to make fun of him. Goliath found out the hard way, as David slew the giant with a small stone and cut off his head with his own sword. The Philistines were shocked and retreated as now Israel's Army was energized and pursued their enemy.

Saul then put David in charge of Israel's defenses, and David was very successful in defeating the Philistines. All seemed to go well until after a great victory Saul overheard the crowd in the city saying, "Saul killed thousands of Philistines while David killed ten thousands." This infuriated Saul, and from that point forward, Saul sought out to kill David. Saul was rejected by God as he had instructed Saul to kill Amalek and to destroy everything in the city and take nothing from it. The Amaleks had previously attacked Israel several times as they left Egypt for the promised land. However, Saul kept some of the best livestock and also preserved the life of Amalek. God had told Samuel, who was the last judge (and was also a priest and prophet), that his blessings and Spirit would leave Saul and that he would anoint another king (which would be King David).

Samuel could do nothing to change God's mind, and the decision was made by God to reject King Saul, and he did. During this entire episode, however, Saul's son, Jonathan, became very close friends with David, and as the hatred grew from his father to David, Jonathan seems to love him even more.

Saul had thrown a spear at David and even ordered him to be killed by some of his men, but David's wife helped him to escape. David's wife Michal was the daughter of King Saul. God has his way of protecting his chosen. While many servants, prophets, and apostles have been persecuted and slain throughout the ages, God has safely delivered them all to the gates of glory in heaven above. We as Christians live in a hostile world that deeply hates us, and many have no idea of why. That hatred is a bit different here in Saul's case, as he was upset that God had rejected him as king, and that resentment was taken out on David. King Saul's jealousy of David was overwhelming and provoked much anger and strife within his family. He just could not get over the favor now God had bestowed upon David.

As humans, it is okay to be angry at times, but the Bible says to "be angry and sin not," and one has to wonder how that can happen. It is all in the motive and intent of the heart that comes into play. Saul sought out to kill the new anointed king and was resentful to the point that it would cost him his life. Saul's relationship between him and his son, Jonathan, became strained as well as Saul didn't want him to befriend David. You are what your friends are. Look at your close friends, and you see a lot of yourself. You do not confide and spend time with those who do not think and act like you like to think and act. It's that simple. Not all church folks are on their merry way to heaven as many of them are wolves in sheep's clothing attacking the sheep and the shepherd behind their backs with their tongue. Yet most of those you find in church are there because they have so much in common which is a result of their faith. You don't work to get faith as work is a result of your faith.

Just as hatred has its own twists and turns, so does love. There is a love a mother has for her newborn that is different than the brotherly love we share in the family of God. Those in church have a deep love for one another, and the source of this love comes from being led by the Spirit of God. There is a love a man has for his wife that is truly a unique love which represents one of the highest degrees of love. We see the love Jonathan had for David, as the scriptures tells us that "he loved him as his own soul." David even was quoted as saying that his love for his friend was that higher than his love for women. This love was beyond all the above and was a love that knit their souls as one and gives a mere glimpse of the love of God he has bestowed upon us. It was an unwavering unselfish love.

During this difficult time, we see the son that could clearly have sided with his father, for his eventual role as king himself, shed the robe of royalty for the friendship of another. How many friends do you have that would do that? We are talking giving up power, money, fine dining, and the best of rides for a mere friendship with a boy his father hated? Yes, Jonathan did just that and will always be remembered for being one of the best role models for a friend in the entire Bible. Jonathan had been victorious in battling the Philistines as well and was well respected in Israel. He could have easily been the next king. Yet he stripped himself of his robe and armor only to give it to David. Remember Jesus stripped himself of his royal robe in heaven only to be ridiculed, smitten, spit upon, and slain on a cross for *his friends*.

Despite Saul's continual hatred toward David, Jonathan tried to reconcile his father toward David, yet Saul refused and even tried to kill Jonathan by throwing a spear at him. Here in the wilderness of Ziph, we see that after discovering his father would not reconcile with David, he gave David the sign to flee, and this was the last time they ever met. Jonathan's father continued the rage in killing David, and while David could have killed Saul, he spared his life as he loved Saul and wished him no harm. It devastated David when Jonathan, Saul, and his entire family were killed by the Philistines. Israel was defeated under Saul's rule, and the Philistines even took the ark of the covenant from Israel.

While this story has a sad ending, we must reflect on this jewel of a friendship, and seriously consider who we are friends with and what kind of friend are we? We need friends like Jonathan, and we need to be a friend like Jonathan to others. Again look at your close friends, and you will get a glimpse of yourself. If you are in the family of God, you need friends that draw you closer to him, not destroy your relationship with him. Listen to their conversation. Listen to their advice. Listen to their dreams. Listen to where they want to spend their time off. Do all these things draw you closer to God?

In closing, I might invite you into a friendship that is like none other as Jesus Christ made one of the most moving statements to his disciples that has always touched my heart,

> **"Henceforth I call you not servants, for the servant knoweth not what his lord doeth: but I have called you friends, for all things that I have heard of my Father I have made known unto you"** (John 15:15).

In my lifetime, I have had the opportunity to meet some fine friends, and some have remained true friends to this day. I call them *true* friends. I have the best and loving family anyone could ask for. I call all of my family my friends. I have a great group of church friends, and they are all special. Again, I consider myself fortunate to have such friends. Yet, I must say that there is no better friend than Jesus Christ. As one gets closer to Christ, he also gets closer to friends that are doing the same. Iron sharpens iron. There are not enough words in the Greek, Aramaic, English, Hebrew, Arabic, and Latin languages to define the love this Man has bestowed upon us. A love even greater than Jonathan's love for David. It's a love worth dying for as our best friend did just that for each one of us that we might be all together upon this earth. I yearn for that day when I can bow down before such a friend and then give him a hug. Yes, I yearn to give my best friend a hug. He's been by my side all the days of my life, and then I can dwell with him forever. For his extended hand of friendship, I have grasped it to never let go. For this, I am forever thankful, and I praise his holy name!

# Chapter 9

## A Journey in the Book of 2 Samuel: The Wisdom of a Woman

> **The matter is not so: but a man of mount Ephraim, Sheba the son of Bichri by name, hath lifted up his hand against the king, even against David: deliver him only, and I will depart from the city. And the woman said unto Joab, Behold, his head shall be thrown to thee over the wall. Then the woman went unto all the people in her wisdom. and they cut off the head of Sheba the son of Bichri, and cast it out to Joan. And he blew a trumpet, and they retired from the city, every man to his tent. And Joan returned to Jerusalem unto the king.**

And the rocks cry out! Abel-beth-maacah is a historical site currently being excavated by the Hebrew University of Jerusalem. I just can't emphasize enough the importance of God giving us so much archeological evidence to prove he and he alone is the author and designer of heaven and earth. On this journey, we get to explore how a woman of great wisdom saves the entire city by her quick thinking and prior knowledge of Israel and her history. Her words were well thought out and her knowledge of Israel ultimately saved the entire city. It is interesting to note the name of this woman was never mentioned, yet her wisdom was certainly appreciated by all within the city gates.

There is some speculation that the woman was perhaps one of Jacob's granddaughters. Regardless of who she was, we know that her wisdom was greatly appreciated in her time.

Just who was threatening this city and why? There was a man named Sheba who was leading a revolt against King David and was on the run, fleeing the army of Israel. Joab was leading David's army and had approached the city and began to dig in to overtake it to get the guilty traitor. We just recently discussed a similar circumstance where an act of evil (gang of men abused and killed a young woman) was committed, and the tribe of Benjamin defended the gang. This resulted in the entire elimination of their great army as they were all defeated. They chose to fight for a bad gang and for the wrong reason.

It is interesting to note how the evil forces backing a revolt of King David's kingdom. Sheba was rebellious toward David and was also from the tribe of Benjamin. Remember that revolt and opposition and many protests are merely Satan's forces influencing and uniting with the spirit of men to rival the kingdom of God and his purpose. God promised another king would come from the descendants of David, and he will ultimately crush Satan with his heel. However, there have been revolts that were led by godly men as we can recall a man named George Washington. He had a God-given vision, and against all odds, the victory came at Yorktown. So the young lion (America) was born. What a blessed nation we are and will be if we continue to support Israel and honor the true and mighty God.

This city's inhabitants, unlike those in the tribe of Benjamin, heeded to wisdom, and the city was preserved by this woman's wise advice as she responded to Joab.

The early church of Ephesus was dear to the apostle Paul's heart as his letter to them is one of his best. The woman in this journey was an exemplary representation of wisdom in her time. Paul, in his letter to the Ephesians, reveals that the wisdom from God was even more revealed in the mystery of Christ. This mystery revealed how the law and the Old Testament prophecy was fulfilled by him. Through Christ's salvation, grace and heirship (Abrahamic promise) was for all. Now through him the reconciliation of the Jews and the Gentiles would be made possible (Ephesians 2). His prayer in chapter 1 is a prayer for all of us:

> **That the God of our Lord Jesus Christ, the Father of glory, may give unto you the spirit of wisdom and revelation in the knowledge of him. The eyes of your understanding being enlightened: that ye may know what is the hope of his calling, and what the riches of the glory of his inheritance in the saints.** (Vs. 17–18)

You see, the woman and Paul, alike, got it. They knew good sound wisdom, and it was reinforced by their knowledge of both God and Christ. The woman said, "Are you not Joab?" Indicating that she knew who he was and also that which he was representing. She knew David would want the city to be offered a treaty of peace in which Joab had not offered. The treaty of peace was traditionally offered to many cities by Israel. Joab and his army had encircled the city, dug in, and was about to tear the walls down. The woman identified herself as an Israelite and Joab's handmaid. This also drew the attention of Joab as he respected her identity and her humility. You never know how much a smile and a gentle answer or even a question can do in a heated situation. The "keep your cool" phrase just might have originated by this wise woman. She worked quickly with the citizens of the city to rally them to deliver what the Israeli Army wanted. It could be debated whether they thought it was the right thing or they merely wanted to avert a siege by the army.

To many it would be a no-brainer, but had they not heeded this woman's advice, the city may have been damaged or destroyed. This army had a reputation of getting things done! So they delivered the head of the traitor, and the city was saved.

There are so many women in the Bible that truly made a difference and were very godly servants. While women and men both have different roles in life, they are equally important in the eyes of God and should be in the eyes of men. God showed his providence and protection for Israel through the life of another famous woman, and that was Esther. Her life too was one of wisdom and knowledge combined to ultimately save Israel. This beautiful woman realized it was her "moment in time" to make a difference for the kingdom of God. She responded to the call even though it was a risk to her life. This is your moment in time. Make a difference in someone's life while you still can. Esther was used by God to save the Jews. I challenge those who are reading to be an instrument to someone in your lives. Be part of pulling them out of the fire. While many who you are on stage with are silently and desperately seeking some sort of deliverance and rescue, you could be the "Esther" in their lives. Be beautiful to somebody as you have truly pleased the Father when you reflect his Son. So let's go back to the days of Esther.

One high-ranking court official, Haman, had secretly devised a plan to kill all of the Jewish people, yet Esther saw through it, and with the help of her cousin, Mordecai, they outwitted the evil man. It was quite fitting that the gallows that Haman had constructed to hang Mordecai were used for him as his evil plot was defeated by the beautiful woman, Esther. The feast of Purim celebrates this great lady and the work and sacrifice she took to save Israel. Her act of approaching the king was one that could have killed her, yet she took a chance and then gained the king's favor. She was truly a beautiful woman that later became queen. There is another story coming soon where a beautiful little boy came, and he too will save Israel in the last days, and he will be King of all kings and Lord of all lords.

> **Therefore the Lord himself shall give you a sign; Behold, a virgin shall conceive, and bear a son, and shall call his name Immanuel.**
> (Isaiah 7:14 KJV)

In closing out this journey, I would like for you to reflect on women and just how much of blessing they are to us. They have a tremendous responsibility as a wife, a mother, a sister, a grandmother and a friend. In many homes throughout the world, she is the only parent caring for her children as well as others. Many women have to work two jobs just to feed their children, and they need to be commended for all of their love and care that comes from being a grandmother, a mother, daughter, a wife, a sister, and a friend. Thank you, each of you, for all of this, and oh yes, thank you for your wisdom.

# Chapter 10

## A Journey in the Book of I Kings: Defeating the Syrian Empire

> **And the king of Israel went out, and smote the horses and chariots, and slew the Syrians with a great slaughter. And the prophet came to the king of Israel, and said unto him, Go, strengthen thyself, and mark, and see what thou doesn't: for at the return of the year the king of Syria will come up against thee.**

It seems like war is discussed in several journeys, and this one concentrates again on an attack on Israel from the Syrians. The tribes of Israel had been divided into two kingdoms. King Solomon's son Rehoboam was now king of Judah, and King Ahab was king of Israel. The Northern Kingdom consisted of all the tribes except Judah and Benjamin. These ten Northern Tribes have been called the lost Tribes of Israel today, yet they are not lost in the eyes of God. Back in their day of division, they chose to rebel and not follow the leadership of David's lineage. This was a mistake as God foretold, through the lineage of David would come a King to an everlasting kingdom that will rule the earth. So the Northern Tribe separated into their own kingdom with its capital in Samaria. Judah's capital remained in Jerusalem.

God has never been pleased with Israel desiring a king in the first place. He rightfully deserved that role. The prophet and priest Samuel warned Israel not to ask for a king. Yet we see in Judges that they did, and the results were not good. They would have been much better had they kept God as their king. Divisions continued as the son of Solomon was not followed by ten of the twelve tribes. The kings of both kingdoms had been often influenced by other gods and self-interests. When a large powerful kingdom divides into smaller states, their vulnerabilities become exposed, which can lead to their eventual defeat. Beware of those creating the deep divisions within our society. The division, in this case, eventually was the culprit that led to their destruction. The Northern Kingdom eventually falls to the Assyrians in 722 BC, and the Southern Kingdom falls to the Babylonians in 586 BC.

It is interesting how this ancient country (Syria) is one of the oldest countries in the Bible, and it still exists today. Damascus still exists today. As Israel would be disobedient and follow other gods, the Aram (Syrian) Army would attack Israel or be dominant over them for a period of time. A good example of this can be found in the third chapter of Judges. In this case, Israel's disobedience cost them eight years of being ruled by the Syrians. There are other confrontations with Syria where God again shows his sovereignty as protector of Israel. Before we visit this Syrian journey, we need to mention another encounter with Israel as one of Israel's prophets had personally become a target of the Syrian Army.

One just never knows just how much warfare is going on in the spiritual realm, in the unseen world, until you observe this story of Syria's army chasing a prophet of God. The Syrian king had devised a plan to attack Israel, and the plan was revealed to Israel by God's prophet Elisha. The king of Syria (Ben Haddad) was furious as he thought he had a spy within his ranks. Yet his officers told him that Elisha was the one who knew the king's personal conversations. The king, instead of realizing he should leave this guy alone, sent a great host after him. The large host then travelled to the city of Dothan, where Elisha and his servant were sleeping, and encircled the city.

When the servant awakened, he was terrified to see the host of Syrian soldiers there.

"What are we going to do?" the servant asked the prophet. The answer Elisha gave this trainee was nothing short of amazing.

He simply said, "Don't worry, kid, we have more on our side than they have on theirs." Then he asked God to show him the unseen world we cannot see. Then God opened the eyes of the servant for just a moment to see the unseen world. There were vast numbers of horses and chariots of fire all around them—which had to be quite a sight to see for this young lad. The story could have ended in total destruction of the host of Syrians, but Elisha simply asked God to blind them. That he did, and then Elisha led them to his city of Samaria, and when they opened their eyes, they were now in their enemy's hands! Here we have the servant experiencing the unseen protection of God, while the enemy sees nothing as they are blindly led into the heart of their enemy's camp. Amazingly Elisha asks for them to be fed and sent home. What an act of mercy to the enemy! This encounter with Syria actually goes into the next book of 2 Kings (chapter 6) but is quite fitting for this journey as we visit the steps of the Syrian Army.

This Syrian journey will take us into one of the battles during King Ahab's reign over Israel. Following Israel's kings is like riding a roller coaster at Cedar Point, as they have victories when they are obedient to God and defeats when they were not. In this war, we see Syria clearly thinks they have the upper hand as they have sent messengers to the king of Israel for specific demands. The Syrian king, Ben Haddad, had gathered a great host of thirty-two kings and a vast army and surrounded Samaria. The messengers he sent into the city asked the king to deliver to the Syrians his gold, silver, his wives, and strong children. King Ahab then agrees to deliver on their demands. It amazes me that the king of Israel offers his family and gold and silver so quickly. However, the Syrian king changes his mind and wants more from the king of Israel. He asks to go throughout the king's house and his servants' houses and take anything they want plus the original demands.

The anxiety had to be overwhelming as the vast army was all around this city, but then a prophet of God shows up. He tells the king that God will give them victory over the huge army. He instructs the young princes to make the advance, and they assemble and attack at noon. King Ben Haddad and his kings are getting quite drunk when the young solders began the attack. The young men and Israel defeated the vast army, yet their Syrian king escaped.

The overconfidence of Israel's enemies can be seen throughout her history as a great thorn in her side, as they cannot see the chariots of fire that is surrounding God's people. Today, Syria is currently in the midst of a civil war, but it appears things are calming down as Assad seems to be winning. He is trying to be diplomatic and make peace with everyone around him. Russia's support of their military and weapons has given Assad the upper hand in the conflict. It appears their direct involvement has now placed Russia more prominently in the geopolitical realm in the Middle East. Syria is an enemy of Israel, and regardless of how diplomatic they may appear, one should not trust the Syrian government in any way. The Bible makes very clear the destiny of those who seek Israel's demise. Just take a look what will happen to Damascus in prophecy, **"The burden of Damascus. Behold, Damascus is taken away from being a city, and it shall be a ruinous heap"** (Isaiah 17:1).

Damascus will be totally destroyed in the future, as prophesied in the Bible. Syria and Assad have close ties to Iran, an obvious enemy of Israel. The annihilation of the Jews will again resurface in the last days, and it will be the climax of Israel's long and rich history. While there is much speculation as to why the Holy Land will become the center of attention in the last days, the answer ultimately is clear. The soon-to-surface antichrist will want to claim to be god and will rule in the Temple in Jerusalem.

> **Who opposeth and exalteth himself above all that is called of God, or that is worshipped; so that he as God sitteth in the temple of God, shewing himself that he is God.** (2 Thessalonians 2:4)

Jacob thought he had trouble back when he was trying to get the love of his life and marry her. Yet Jacob's (Israel) real trouble could soon be on the horizon. Many governments today are meeting as we speak, devising plans for the destruction of Israel and the Jewish people. It is the same evil spirit inspiring current leaders that motivate people, groups, and governments that existed since Abraham received his promise from God.

While it is true that there is nothing new under the sun, it must be understood that the level of intensity of the rise of evil will be unsurpassed in human history as those forces realize their final days are drawing near. (Daniel 12:1). It appears the upheaval of evil we are witnessing throughout the world may be yet another sign we are near the last days prophesied in the Bible. As this intensity of evil grows, then division and separation of multitudes will assemble themselves on the world stage.

> **But beloved, remember ye the words which were spoken before of the apostles of our Lord Jesus Christ; How that they told you there should be mockers in the last time, who should walk after their own ungodly lusts. These be they who <u>separate themselves</u>, sensual, having not the Spirit. (Jude 1:17–19).**

This division is growing day by day in the world. Call it the far-left liberals or what you may, but it is simply those believing the lies of evil and vehemently defending it. It's literally a mass gathering of those in their circle, and their motive is driven by Satan himself. Don't blame a party nor the far-left liberals for all of this, simply be patient with those opposing the truths of God as they are deep in the sea of darkness drawn by chains and weights that Satan has wrapped them in. These blinded people need our prayers as we interact with them every day. Those demanding tolerance are becoming intolerant, and the division in their soul begins to overtake their minds. God says these people will believe a lie in the last days, and they will be led by strong delusion. The lust of the flesh and of this world that drew Israel away from God has blinded them as well:

> **So, I gave them up unto their own hearts' lust: and they walked in their own counsels.** (Psalm 81:12)

While this scripture dips into Israel's punishment for denying, rebelling and being disobedient to God, it also applies to all those living in the last days.

> **And with all deceivableness of unrighteousness in them that perish because they received not the love of the truth, that they might be saved. And for this cause, God shall send them strong delusion, that they should believe a lie.** (2 Thessalonians 2:10–12)

In the last days (after the rapture), the enemies's persecution and triumph over believers will seem secure until the Son of God arrives with his army of saints from heaven (Revelation 19:14–15). Again remember the rapture is when Christ comes *after* his bride and his next appearance is seven years later *with* his bride as he destroys the armies surrounding Israel. Somewhere in there, we see the total destruction of Damascus, and it will be total destruction. The total destruction of Damascus prophesied in Isaiah simply means you can throw Assad and all those he is currently courting into the ring of those secretly and openly seeking the final solution. Yet while Hitler's persecution and atrocities actually permitted God's people to return and establish their country, the antichrist will usher in his own final defeat and cause the final redemption of Israel to be completed. Hitler ultimately paved the way for Israel to return to their homeland, and the antichrist will pave the way for the King of kings to return to the homeland forever.

Now we will move on to our next journey in 2 Kings.

# Chapter 11

## A Journey in the Book of 2 Kings: A Sign from God

**And Hezekiah slept with his fathers: and Manasseh his son reigned in his stead. Manasseh was twelve years old when he began to reign, and fifty and five years in Jerusalem. And his mother's name was Hephzibah.**

While we see Manasseh was one of the evil kings and did evil in the eyes of God, we will direct our attention to King Hezekiah and his relationship with God.

If you haven't noticed, I refer to the discovery of artifacts to be just one of God's ways of proving himself. I once saw a photograph of a sign beside the road that read "*If you are looking for a sign from God, this is it.*" I loved that image as it is so true for so many people. It seems many are looking for answers to the problems facing us in America and abroad. Some are looking for signs or just some message from God. You could quite well just be getting that as you travel on each of these journeys. While most of these journeys takes us back into time, others take us into today's world, and even into each of our futures. Yet there is no new revelation that will come from this book, as God has revealed everything we need to know about our future in the scriptures.

The message of God and the Holy Scriptures were completed on the isle of Patmos back in 95 AD. Yet the folks living on the earth now are living in the best of times. While many debate the timing of the Rapture (departure) and even go to extremes to fighting and arguing over such timing, others are content in their lives as they have been deep into the meat of the Word and are living life to its fullest. These people are ready to meet the Lord at any moment should he return. Be in the few who are in this circle. Healthy debate is fine, yet fighting and arguing among the brethren should not exist among the mature Christians. There is still so much for us to learn and know as we search the scriptures, and while prophecy should be studied, the message of salvation should always be our main objective. That is because it is Christ's main objective. Again, be strong in the Lord by studying his Word as Christ lives within our heart. Jesus said in Matthew 12 that out of the heart of a good man comes good things and out of an evil heart comes evil things (verse 35). Not only does he know the Word of God but he is also living in his word and striving to know him and his love. If you recall the Psalm 91 scripture I recalled while I was covered up in the coal mine, look carefully at verses 14 to 15.

> **Because he hath set his love upon me, therefore will I deliver him: I will set him on high, because he hath known my name. He shall call upon me, and I will answer him: I will be with him in time of trouble; I will deliver him, and honour him.** (Psalm 91:14–15)

You see, we must set our love upon our Father and we must seek to know him. Then he hears our cry, he hears our pleas, and he hears our smallest prayers. As the stage is now set for the wrath and "trouble" as we have never seen, you will be delivered, my friend, and be honored in the kingdom of heaven. Bathe yourself in his promises in these days of uncertainty, and encourage one another with the hope that rests deep within you. With the love of God in your heart, cherish each day, and let that love and light shine among all those around you. The world needs your hope, your smile, and your faith.

The stage on earth was made by God, and while the names of the actors may change, the setting remains the same here on planet Earth. You are on stage now. Stories of old need to be told to our children of God's power and love. Stories of our own experiences need to be told to all of God's love and power. Stories need to be made. "God's will be done" is in the Lord's prayer, and it will be done. That is when his kingdom comes to the earth forever. That story has yet to happen, but the events leading to that are at our doorstep. This journey about Hezekiah comes at a time when a recent excavation in Jerusalem has found proof of this king's existence by a seal with his inscription on it. Yes, the stones are crying out. He lives! Looking for a sign? That is a good one to look up. We will also visit this king's request for a sign from God that is unique as well as my own personal request(s).

As I mentioned earlier in my introduction, I have seen the hand of God working in the lives of family members as well as others most of my life. I am quite embarrassed to say that at times, I too have asked God to do some particular thing so that I might have an answer from him. There has never been any doubt of God's existence in my entire lifetime. I was, by no means, testing God in each of these circumstances; nor was I trying to make any deal with God. I could write on and on how I've seen his hand at work in my lifetime, but the story of the three bucks is one truly for the ages. Get your hunting gear on and dress warmly as this is quite an exciting ride.

These events may offend some as I must reveal to you that I once was an avid deer hunter. I enjoyed bowhunting as well as gun and muzzleloader hunting. I still hunt somewhat today, but I enjoy the fellowship with being with my brothers at deer camp more than actually killing those beautiful animals.

## The Ten-Pointer Sign

***The sign from God to the atheist.*** One of my roommates in college was a dedicated atheist (we will call him John). It was opening morning of deer season (1982) in Randolph County, West Virginia, that I thought of this guy. We had several discussions before my hunting trip on the existence of God while in our dorm room at Fairmont State University. I can recall standing on a stump on that cold opening day as I was praying for my family's safety during the hunting season. I then thought of John and simply prayed that God would send me a ten-point buck to kill so that John would know that he existed. To ask for and actually bag such a trophy buck would most definitely require an act of God. I was eating corn nuts up a deep hollow when a beautiful buck came into sight, deep within the hollow. I was calm at first, as I was admiring the tall white tines on this large buck. I then broke a twig and spooked it, and it then began running. My heart was pounding as I squeezed a shot off with it running. They call it the buckacres here in the mountains!

I was greatly disappointed as I thought that I had missed the buck. I followed the deer's tracks to a heavily covered slope, and there he jumped up, and I fired several times to drop the beautiful animal. His rack was tall and white and a hunter's dream. I rushed down the hill, and my brother Randy, who was nearby, came around the hill toward the deer. When I got to the buck, I quickly began counting the points, and I counted one, two, three, four, five, six, seven points. But then lying beside the rack were three more as I had shot three of them off! My brother Mark later glued them back on. Now to some, this may be just good luck, but there was no luck involved. The story and the antlers made it back to my roommate and other friends, and the story did impress the guy. I cannot tell you if "John" ever made a commitment to God. It has been my prayer that this miracle by God would move him to the saving grace of Jesus Christ.

*The Seven-Pointer*

*The sign from God for my calling.* In the beautiful hills of Pendleton County, West Virginia, on a cold November morning in 1991, a seven-point buck was lying on the ground as another sign from God. I asked God for a sign, before season opened, for him to send me a seven-point buck as knowing that he was calling me into his ministry. I had felt his hand upon me long before this, yet in my weakness, I still wanted to have a "sign" from God. Seven is the perfection number from God, and it took me quite a while to realize the ten-point buck, that was a sign to the atheist, was actually for me as well. It was a seven point when I first saw it as I had shot three points off of its rack! Wow. God gave me a preview of my calling with the ten-pointer, then the miracle of the seven-pointer in Pendleton County, West Virginia. While I ponder why the Creator of the universe would take time to call me in such a way was quite humbling then and still is today. I must say, all of this attention God gave me was by, in no way, for my benefit but for the benefit of others. I had joy in my life, yet it became *abundant* joy when I saw both the ten-pointer and the seven-pointer lying on the earth. They were there, in that point in time, not so much for me but that *you might know* that same abundant joy that comes only from the Father.

*The Eight-Pointer*

*The sign from God to my family.* While driving to our camp in Randolph County, just before buck season, I was driving on Turkey Bone Road when I was praying again for safety for my family before the shooting began. I thought of just how blessed I was to have such a wonderful family, and I said, "Lord, please show my brothers just how much you love them and that you want to be closer to them. To show them that you're on the throne and that you love them, let me kill an eight-point buck." I was hunting below the bridge in Silica, on the right side of the mountain, when the eight-pointer made its way in my sights, and it was over for that beautiful animal as well. It was a sign from God, again not only to my family but for everyone reading this book. It wasn't an earth-moving event, but the answered prayer was so profound. To know God, you must understand family. God wants you to be in his family. There are just so many people that just needs to know that God is on his throne and that he deeply loves you! That is why God created you and me! His love goes beyond our understanding as its depth and height have no end. It is very clear now that the first sign (ten pointer) was an event from God for all those who need a sign to ensure his existence and his sovereignty. He is God, and there is none other. The second sign (seven pointer) was for all of you reading this book to know that I have been chosen by God himself to write this book, and he and he alone gave me the task and the ability to write the contents within this reading. He prepared me for thirty years after my calling to write the message this book contains. While there are no "new revelations" within this book, it contains content that needs to be remembered, cherished, and dwelled upon as we are living in a crucial time in human history. The time for the church and its purpose is nearing its end. Many call this time the dispensation of grace that we are now living and despite all the chaos and confusion that exists today, this book is to show many that there is hope, there is peace, and there is joy. There is another day for those who love the Lord. In fact, there is an eternity of joy for those in his family. The door of getting this book done was opened by God, and I am blessed to be able to get it finished. His calling me is a vital point that has to be understood as you continue reading this book. I apologize for not being an English major as the writing style and grammar may be rough around the edges, but to the point. While the eight-point buck was a sign sent to my brothers, it was also for all of us. We all must know that God is on the throne and that he deeply loves each one of us. He deeply desires fellowship with you.

Therefore, by these signs, our Creator of the universe took the time to reveal once again his love for *you* through these events in my life. He was not just calling me, my friend, but also calling you.

Now we go to the sign from God as we see the life and death of King Hezekiah. We know from the scriptures that this king did what was right in the eyes of God. We get a glimpse of a king that got rid of all the idols and those leaders of those false gods during his reign. It is interesting to note this king was told by the prophet Isaiah that he was to get his house in order because he was about to die. The king (like most of us) wanted to live longer, so he pleaded and prayed for an extension of his life. God later told Isaiah that he would answer the king's prayer and give him fifteen more years of life. When the king was told this, he wasn't convinced, so he asked for a sign from God. So King Hezekiah requested the earth reverse its orbit as this would be quite a task! God did just that again, not so much for this king but for all of us. (II Kings 20:11) Now reversing the earth's orbit is quite a sign!

It has been reported that both astronomers as well as NASA has verified the earth has lost a day in the researched history of our universe. You can also read in the story of Joshua (10:13) where the sun was stopped for nearly a day during a battle in Israel. Many scholars feel both this event and the forty-minute sign for King Hezekiah make up the lost day the astronomers refer to. Whether you want to believe these reports are up to you, as it is amazing how God has given us the means to check him out, and he will prove himself by the present and the past. Therefore, we must take into careful consideration that he knows and *will ultimately control* the future and *our future*.

Many ask for a sign from God when it is already there. A friend, a family member, a stranger, or maybe a book is staring you right in the face. If you don't recognize them immediately, take a moment to sit down and watch a sunrise or a sunset. A true painting made by the hands of God. It is not just a sign but an invitation to fellowship with him.

# Chapter 12

## A Journey in the Book of 1 Chronicles: Derailing a King

**And David said unto Gad, I am in a great strait: let me fall now into the hand of the LORD; for very great are his mercies: but let me not fall into the hand of man. So the LORD sent pestilence upon Israel: and there fell of Israel seventy thousand men.**

Scriptures tell us and it is no secret that King David was truly one flawed guy as he was a murderer, an adulterer, and at times, a proud and arrogant king. Then you want to ask yourself, is this the guy that God promised that through his lineage would come the Messiah and the King of all kings?

As we opened this book, you will recall the opening comments on how the human race has fallen deeply into the abyss of darkness of placing value on the valueless. Yet we must never mistake the value God has in your faith in him. You see, while even the most despicable crimes of murder and adultery are two of God's most hated sins, he will forgive you for them, just as He forgave King David. Not only that, he can still take that old clay while it's on the pedestal and mold it yet again into a beautiful and useful vessel. We should never be critical of those that have fallen in life. Those drawing closer to God get more attention from our enemy than anyone else. Satan will fire at will at those making a difference in the spiritual realm of life. He is out to destroy those drawing near to God. He takes great pleasure in attacking God's children through weak Christians as well as those easily swayed into his onslaught of attacks.

The Bible is full of imperfect people struggling against this foe, and we are no exception as we continue the faith. We are attacked daily by Satan as life is a struggle. Faith in God never presents smooth sailing but keeps us afloat in a sea of darkness. As now the hand of God has pulled us to safety into the ship of Zion. Yet the seas are still rough, and the waves are raging, and while we may get seasick, we will never drown. There is not a storm that Jesus cannot calm the waters. Just remember, Satan always throws temptations and ill will toward any servant of God. It is bad enough when those following Satan begins to tear apart God's people, yet it gets even worse when one gets shot in the back by his own brothers and sisters in Christ. When we begin to judge and criticize others, that same judgment will fall back on yourself. So many detrimentally criticize others sins and faults merely because they differ from their own.

God had foretold the prophet Samuel that David would be king of Israel. Yet God knew David would fail even at that time, but he knew David would truly repent and get back up and fight another day. God led that little known shepherd boy to unite and lead the nation of Israel. Faith in God never provides a bed of roses, as this journey reveals. Yet always remember, as you study the life of King David, that God says that he was a man after his own heart. That says a lot and is something to consider before one ridicules a pastor or choir member or a family member when they stumble. A true brother or sister is there to pick you up and help you along the way. Beware of those who have an empty quiver, having emptied it on their own brothers and sisters. I assure you that God will hold those accountable.

These journeys are also a means to strengthen the church. I encourage those that have been critical of others to immediately stop and be an encourager to, first of all, your brothers and sisters in Christ. Secondly, be sensitive to others as you never walked in their shoes. By *showing love and forgiveness*, you can represent the best of what Jesus stands for. It will be mentioned numerous times in this book, and I cannot overemphasize it enough, as Jesus said, the greatest commandment is "to love the LORD thy God, with all thy heart and with all thy soul and with all thy mind." The next greatest commandment actually is not so difficult if one follows the first one. The second greatest commandment is to "love thy neighbor as thyself." The more you love God, the better friend you are capable of being. It's tough spending any amount of time around someone who never cracks a smile. Smile and take your hand and give a struggling brother or sister a hug, not an arrow in the back. Take the high road and be a light unto others. You have the light as you are reflecting Christ, so use it to lead others out of despair and darkness.

This journey is about a king who has made a mistake by numbering those in Israel without following the rules God had made for a census (Exodus 30). This is not the first time King David made a mistake and was certainly not his last. This small act of disobedience, however, cost the lives of seventy thousand men. There are many instances in life that we blame Satan for the temptation or the act of disobedience when actually, it is merely the selfish flesh that is making the call. As discussed earlier, one must realize that the hardships and struggles we endure here on earth is a preparation for our blessings and reward to come. We must never forget that God chastens his own. In this case with King David, we see the king being attacked by Satan and the consequences of David's decision. In this journey, we observe Satan again creating chaos in the nation of Israel. This is another attack from the devil himself. Those in the frontlines of the battle are the ones he shoots at and with all that he has. God's leaders always tend to be his biggest target who, in this case, is King David. Satan provoked David to hastily take a census of Israel as David did, but David failed to follow God's instructions on taking the census. While there are so many lessons from the Holy Scriptures that we can study and keep within, this perhaps should be one kept near your heart and mind and soul.

Always be aware that your acknowledgment, desire, and walk with God will be met each and every time by two enemies: self and Satan. Each and every adult soul ultimately chooses their pathway daily which takes them to eternity. As humans, we all are on the same level. There is no place in heaven or the new earth for pride, racism, or arrogance as these are Satan's tools for division. We all face temptations, trials, and hardships of life.

Mountains and valleys, rivers and streams are crossed. Storms rage on only to see the beauty of the earth cleansed and a gorgeous rainbow of promise painted in the sky by God himself. One pathway is wide and so many are along the way appearing to be satisfied, but it is only temporary. Yet the other pathway less traveled is narrow, but it leads us straight to the gates of heaven. Satan's forces are in full mode of derailing those on the narrow pathway so others may question their struggles as a way of questioning the God they serve. While those on the narrow road constantly face stumbling blocks which they encounter along the way, Satan misconstrues these struggles as a weakness and lack of faith. I am sure King David had many throughout his life who were quick to ridicule and judge him as he stumbled and fell. But don't forget the Goliaths who also fell at the hands of David. When God is first, the giants fall.

Many find fault in King David for not only making a hasty bad choice on this journey but for committing adultery and murder as well. David was in the middle of a great spiritual battle in which he fell, but then he got up, repented, and moved on. The pattern continues as many called of God have been mocked for their mistakes as they too had fallen. I'm not condoning their actions as there were consequences for each failure but rewards as well. The prize, my friend, comes from getting up with a new day in front of you as you get on your knees in prayer and move closer to our Creator. Our main reward is forgiveness—complete forgiveness after true repentance has been made.

Consider the psalms that David wrote and the good that he did for Israel. If you look closely, you can see the pattern in the psalms closely related to this journey. You will see the offense, the reaction, the consequences, the repentance, and then the moving on to a new day and a better day. That, my friend, is the life of the children of God. To all of those who promise a bed of roses for following God, it is a grave mistake and a false stumbling block to many. The Bible is full of people, rich and poor, struggling, being persecuted, beaten, crucified, mocked, neglected, and ridiculed who were close to God. If you were to ask them now while they are now in the presence of God, they would assure you to keep the faith and stay on course as your reward is beyond words and beyond description.

While I have not physically heard those in eternity, it is as if their message both from heaven and hell is resonating to us in some of these journeys. Many of you reading this book have loved ones that have gone on before you, and they want the message of this book to motivate you and move you from where you are. Again don't ask me to judge King David nor anyone else in my life, but I will confirm everyone will meet and answer to the Judge, Jesus Christ. The Word of God says every knee shall bow and every tongue confess that Jesus is Lord. This verse is proof that there will be no atheists on that day. Remember, God and Jesus chastises those who go astray as we clearly see in both Testaments of the Bible. Those facing judgment have totally rejected God and his Son and must face eternal judgment.

Here we see the chastisement of King David. David was given three options that the prophet Gad revealed for his disobedience (we usually do not get a choice!). David chose the last option which would be delivered by God and not by man. David's reasoning was that God would possibly show more mercy than his enemy would. The other two options of three years of famine or three months of his enemy having victory over him and his army, were passed over and pestilence sent by God, was chosen by the king. The pestilence was worse than David imagined as the adult men began dying by the thousands due to the pestilence. The angel of the Lord told the prophet Gad to have David build an altar of sacrifice. David quickly paid the landowner for the property to build the altar and made the altar and the sacrifice so that God would stop the pestilence on Israel.

This journey has taken us to a great king and his experience of being idle in the crosshairs of the enemy. When one is constantly reading God's Word, attending church functions, and serving others in the church and on the street, the enemy has trouble hitting the target. A moving target is tough to hit. Yet when the object stops, the target is easily hit and often hit hard. It wasn't the first time that David was tempted by Satan and lured by his selfish desires. Yet one must note that in reverence and fear of the *Lord*, David not only reacted quickly, but he truly repented for his poor judgment, which resulted in the pestilence being stopped. Yet don't forget that seventy thousand households were without a father or a brother as the result of his failure.

The family of God includes those who are at the foot of the cross as well as those who have fallen and rolled down the hill. Yet they are both forgiven as they have placed their faith in the finished work of the Son of God and nothing else. All Christians have walked the narrow path with various levels of maturity and closeness to God. My hat is off to those who daily seek to draw nigh to God. I encourage those who spend most of their free time holding a phone in their hand to get the Bible app and read the good news and the social media from the gates of glory. As true believers, we all stumble and fall. Some more than others, and again we need to be an encourager when one stumbles. Pick 'em up! As those who stumble from sickness, from financial woes, from a job loss or a divorce, or from a bad relationship, or any other baggage, we need to forgive the guy "seventy times seven," as Christ commanded to each of us.

How can you possibly hold a grudge against someone and have an unforgiving spirit when you expect Christ to wipe all your past and present transgressions off the books? I mean, seriously? As the guy rolls down the hill with his failure, just watch as it is just a matter of time that he will stop, get up, and head back up that mountain. His focus is on the cross which stands alone for his prize. It's the prize already given, but the sacrifice was made by the one who hung upon it. All believers acknowledge the vastness of the debt we have and are totally unable to repay. Yet the huge ransom was paid on that cross. That cross was the hope the prophets of old looked so forward to, and now we look back as it rests upon the top of the mountain. Keep your focus on the top of the mountain regardless of your position in life. Remember all true Christians have turned from the wide worldly road, to the hill of Golgotha.

Again, some crawl, some walk, and some sprint, but each time they get up from the fall, they focus on the cross and start back up the mountain. All those in the family, mature and babes included, have been cleansed by the ultimate sacrifice made on the cross. We ask for forgiveness as we are reminded of the cross and our faith is in him and not of anything else. Our failure is gone, and the blood has cleansed us and granted us a righteous garment that has been made for us in heaven.

Faith in God involves a mindset that only comes from the heart. The substance that the heart and soul possess directly drives the mindset of each person on earth. The heart and soul have welcomed the Holy Spirt of God to dwell there. The Holy Spirit then changes the entire mindset of the human spirit. This mindset is always acknowledging that we have fallen or are falling, and only by a repentant state of mind can we please God. Our faith in *his* means of cleansing is our ticket to heaven. This entire process is called sanctification. We begin our sanctification when we first put our faith in the finished work of the Son of God. This process involves all the hills we have rolled down and focusing again on the cross at the top of the mountain. God has set us apart and written our names in the Book of Life with the blood of his Son.

Our sanctification is completed when we are given our new bodies promised by God that will then occupy our hearts and soul forever and ever. Many have asked how old will our bodies look like when we get them? Some have said thirty-three, as this was the age of Christ when he was crucified and conquered death. I am not sure, but I am sure of one thing, and that is we will all be known by one another when we are in heaven and on the new earth.

This has been a great journey, and now we will move on to our next one in 2 Chronicles.

# CHAPTER 13

## A Journey in 2 Chronicles: Singing on Earth and in Heaven

**And when they began to sing and to praise, the LORD set ambushments against the children of Ammon, Moab, and mount Seir, which were come against Judah; and they were smitten.**

What song is in your heart today? Needless to say, songs tend to stick with us, and there is nothing wrong of reminiscing the good ole songs of your youth. Music can invoke many emotions and good memories. In this journey, we see the act of singing prompted the Lord of Hosts to move and take action. Judah was in trouble, and a vast army had sailed over and threatened to annihilate all of God's people. To prepare ourselves for this journey, we must go to the lands of Ammon, Moab, and Mount Seir (Esau's descendants). These enemies of Israel had assembled a great army. King Jehoshaphat (Israel's king) prayed during Israel's time of fear, and his prayer is quite intriguing.

As we look into his prayer, we note some very interesting points that should be made about this prayer. First, he reminded God how he had delivered them into the land he promised Abraham, and how God had previously heard their cry in past trials, pestilences, wars, and judgments. Therefore, through all they have been through, Jehoshaphat pleaded with God to please come to their rescue. The answer from God came through a man named Jahaziel, as the Spirit of the Lord came upon him. His word from God was one for the ages as God told the king of Judah

> **"Not to be afraid nor dismayed for the battle is not yours, but God's"** (2 Chronicles 20:15).

These invaders of Jerusalem now have no chance of victory with a statement like that from the Lord of Hosts. All of Jerusalem were relieved to hear this, and they all gathered and began praising the Lord.

The next morning, the praising continued as they began preparations to confront the enemy. This was a huge army and was strategically placed for battle when Jehoshaphat gave the command that we all must heed in time of battle,

> **"Believe in the Lord your God, so shall ye be established; Believe his prophets, so shall ye prosper"** (20:20).

So here we are, witnessing again a massive group assembled by the enemies of Israel going to great lengths to assemble the army from Moab, Ammon, and Mount Seir (Esau's descendants). We have, and will continue discussing how the enemies of Israel continues their quest to destroy this tiny nation of God's chosen people. Battles have been won and battles were lost, yet *the* war has been won. Yet a remnant of God's people have always been preserved and protected by God.

The Old Testament flows in great beauty into the New Testament as the old covenant moved into a new one when the Son of God showed up on earth. The battles against God's people will remain until the final one we will visit in the last book of the Bible. One must consider the headlines today as the same spirit that was moving all of these armies against Israel back then are still at work today. Many countries have courted Israel and befriended them only to arrive later with their invading armies. The Bible is full of assurances, however,

Israel will never be wiped off the map, and all those opposing her will be destroyed.

How any leader or soldier could march against the holy city of Jerusalem is beyond me. In this case, the king assembled a group of singers at the battle front lines, and they began singing. They sang from their hearts. They praised the God of the Most High. They were praising him in heart and soul and mind and in spirit. It was no ordinary day and no ordinary singing. They were, in fact, praising him for the victory that had already been won. Israel still has more battles ahead of her in the near future as Russia, Turkey, Iran and Syria will be assembling an army just as Moab, Ammon, and Esau's descendants did in this journey. I assure you that all of this vast army, as well as all future armies of the world combined, will be defeated as the battles rage on. However, just as these singers were assured by God himself, Israel can be assured she will *win the war.*

Israel will win because the war is actually the Lord's and not that of Israel. The powers of the air and spiritual wickedness is driving all of this hatred and while the land of Israel is a target of the enemy, it is all those that love and honor God that they seek to wound and destroy. Choose this day who you will fight for. While spiritual forces are the actual driver for war, we as humans fight ferociously with all of our means, from swords to hypersonic weapons now at our disposal. Yet no weapon has any strength against the Lord of lords and King of kings (Psalm 2).

There is no safe place now on earth that a nuclear weapon cannot reach and utterly wipe out. Yet we must consider the real players here, and it all boils down to the kingdom of God versus the kingdom of evil. Satan and his evil forces are of no match to us humans as he, as a fallen angel, has enough power and persuasion to convince a third of heaven to follow him. His power is real and really deceiving, to say the least. Though he was created by God, and while his power is overwhelming to us at times, it is by no means a rival to God. We are overcomers of Satan by the authority given to us through Christ.

**Behold, I give unto you power to tread on serpents and scorpions, and over all the power of the enemy: and nothing shall by any means hurt you.** (Luke 10:19)

Remember there is power (wonder-working power) in the spoken word of God and the finished work of his Son.

But never underestimate the influence Satan has upon the earth. Just look around. Just as we see such a mess it is, remember the guy who has all the toys will renew it and enjoy it with those who love him and sing to him! Every person has a song in their heart. Listen to good music that gives glory, honor, praise, and thanksgiving to the Man who made this all possible—the Son of God!

It is so amazing to go into this place on this journey and take a moment to see these singers and how their admiration and praise to God pulled the trigger to defeat the enemy. I can almost hear their singing as the victory has been won. "Oh Victory in Jesus" would have been my favorite, though he had not arrived quite yet. I am sure it would have been so moving to have heard these praises going up to the heavens. When God saw that his people, who were deep in fear the day before, were now truly trusting in him, truly and deeply praising him, he responded quickly. The enemies simply turned on one another, and the war turned away from those in Jerusalem to a fight within themselves. They literally all killed one another.

The king of Israel and all their army found their enemies slaughtered, and it took three days to haul off all of the food, gold, and valuables that these invaders had at their camp. Apparently, all of those soldiers forgot their history lesson of Pharaoh's people giving God's people so much and to leave Egypt. God inspired the Egyptian people to find favor in His people, and they took their wealth with them (Genesis 12:36). They forgot how all those Egyptian soldiers that persecuted and pursued the Jews were all drowned in the Red Sea. As discussed earlier, the Triune of God represents so many things, humility being one at the top. Yet there are times where the will of God is so neglected, ignored, and even confronted by man that he takes action (some call judgment) to make a point. He intervened numerous times, in the history of Israel, to pass judgment, to prove his existence, and to prove himself, not only to them but to the enemy as well. The enemies of God have heard or read the stories of God sending in the cavalry and giving his people a victory. Yet somehow they still move and chose to reject God (John 12:48) and to fight, rebel, and create chaos against those faithful and loyal to God. God revealed to man rules to live by and we are now experiencing the prophecies today where those laws and rules are disrespected and ignored. This spirit of lawlessness paves the way for a false leader and prophet to arise and make his own laws. The deceiver finally gets his moment in time. In the end, God's patience and dispensation of grace will end, and those refusing and rebelling against his authority will be given over to the deceiver's leader and his lieutenants. The scriptures are clear we are rapidly nearing the days of judgement which will take the world by storm. There is a spirit of lawlessness taking hold here in America that is growing exponentially and is yet another sign we are clearly living in the latter days. If you bundle all these folks up that God addresses in the last days, you might take note and consider where you stand as we are nearing this time.

- Those looking for the Son of God to return—These are the five virgins that have their lamps trimmed and burning and watching for the bridegroom to come after his bride (the faithful church). You need to be in this group.
- Those who claim to be Christians and Jews by name only. Their mouths speak of good things, yet their heart, soul, and spirit have refused the Spirit of God. You don't want to be in this group.
- Those who have forgotten God. The love they once had for him and his provisions, safety, and blessings have been forgotten and put on the back burner. Life is good for them and little-to-no need for a close relationship with God. You don't want to be in this group. These groups are defined in the seven churches in Revelation. Look them up when you have time. Be in the church of Philadelphia. There will be no "secret" Christians taken in the depar-

ture for the Marriage Supper of the Lamb. Have you ever heard of a bride spending her entire life never mentioning the name of her groom? Jesus makes it perfectly clear that "if you don't mention me on earth, then I won't mention you in heaven." It's just that simple. The call is made to all those who are worthy. The response is only made by the faithful.

- Those who have committed themselves wholly to the world system and claim to be anything but a follower of God or of his Son. While all the above need prayer, these folks need it the most. These souls openly and vehemently oppose God and those who even have an inkling of affection for him. Beware of the agenda these folks have as they are serving Satan and hate those who do not follow him (Luke 16:13). Serve God and not money.
- The twelve tribes of Israel—The last days, yes, is to bring judgment to the earth and for the final redemption of Israel to take place. I encourage all Jewish folks to accept Jesus now. Conditions will get to where you will later on. Choose him now before the seals in Revelation are broken.
- Satan's empire—God makes it clear that Satan will have his moment in time to be praised by man as he sets up his kingdom on earth. He will even sit as god on his throne in the temple in Jerusalem (Daniel 9:27; 2 Thessalonians 2:3–4; Revelation 13:5–7). Yet it will not end well for Satan and all of his followers (Revelation 19:11-21). If you are living on earth as this is happening, never take his mark and never serve him. Those taking the mark of the beast will fall under the direct wrath of God. His destiny should not be yours.
- Those who will be martyred during Satan's short reign on earth (Revelation 15:1–3). These are the ones that hope to get right with God yet miss the departure of those true to him. There are many, and while it may be controversial to some, many will be saved during the tribulation time. If not so, then many scriptures must be taken out of the Bible. I

cannot do that. Just as the Jew can make things right, so can you before the judgment of God begins. Again, I judge no one, and neither should you. God knows the heart and motives of the human heart. The scriptures are perfectly clear that one has to be worthy to be taken in the departure. All that is required is faith in Him. Enough faith to watch for and love his appearing.

Yet, many will be too busy and tuned in to the world and will get caught in the snare that will come upon the entire world. Many will go into the tribulation who will turn to Christ, yet they will be killed for their testimony for Christ. Remember, he comes as a thief in the night for his bride; and many of those left will be startled, utterly shocked, and deeply remorseful.

As we consider those who have been killed for their testimony (Revelation 15:1–3), for their stand for God and refusing Satan's mark, we notice the scene here in heaven—they are singing the song of Moses *and* the song of the Lamb as this further defines both Jew and Gentile will be saved during the great tribulation. These folks are singing their hearts out as their persecution, torture, and ridicule is over, and they are now rejoicing in heaven! You can see they have truly accepted the Lamb of God (final redemption). The singing of the song of Moses and their realization of the truth of Christ opened their eyes on earth during this time of great tribulation. They realize he was the Messiah all along. Their acceptance of the true Messiah has gotten them to the glorious gates of heaven, and now they have seen him face-to-face. They have seen his nail-scarred hands. They are anxiously awaiting the time they can join their completed fellow Jews that still remain on earth. They too, at this time, will be looking for his coming to deliver them from the deceiver. That day will arrive. Then there will be singing! Oh, what shouting! Oh, what singing on that happy morning!

The battle for Jerusalem, while it is currently being planned out, will have its final day. When it is over, I assure you that there will be singing in that land. This promise is in Isaiah chapter 14:7, "**The whole earth is at rest, and is quiet: they break forth into singing.**"

I can see the choir in that old Baptist church I was raised from my early childhood. I can still hear my mother's voice above all others singing. I can see her smile and her joy as she sang praise to the Most High God and to his Son. These songs stayed with me as well as the memories of that old church atmosphere. I can still see and hear her singing "Oh, Victory in Jesus" in that ole Baptist Church in Leivasy, West Virginia. When you have a moment, pull up these songs as they are some of my favorites: "It's Shouting Time in Heaven" by the Hoppers. "Beulah Land" by Squire Parsons. "Midnight Cry" by Ivan Parker. "God on the Mountain" by Lynda Randle. "Go Rest High on That Mountain" by Vince Gill. "Silent Night" by Kelly Clarkson, Trisha Yearwood, and Reba McEntire.

Also include "The Little Drummer Boy" by Pentatonix as that song truly says we have nothing to really give back to our Savior, but a song. A song of praise, my friend. He loves it when we sing and play music for him. Just ask King David. I love to sing and do, mostly when I am by myself! I have a rough voice and cannot carry a tune if I had to. Yet, I still sing Christmas songs in July, and while many say it's not Christmas, I reply, "Oh yes, it is, every day is Christmas!" Because all is calm, and all is bright, and it is great to sleep in heavenly peace. Sing and give praise to God as he inhabits and camps about those who love and think upon his name. Be in his book of Remembrance. (Malachi 3:16)

Even so, come, Lord Jesus. Oh yes, just another song to enjoy and look up: "Even so come Lord Jesus" by Kristian Stanfill.

Now we will journey on into the book of Job to visit the falsely accused.

# Chapter 14

# A Journey in the Book of Job: The Falsely Accused

**There shall be none of his meat left; therefore shall no man look for His goods. In the fulness of His sufficiency, He shall be in straits: Every hand of the wicked shall come upon Him.**

We had an earlier journey describing what a true friend Jonathan was to David. Just as there are those that are closer than a brother or sister in life, we unfortunately have those Zophars that exist as well. Here, like David, we see a direct attack on one of God's servants, Job. In this journey, we are brought to a visit from Job's friend, Zophar.

Zophar was one of the three friends that had come to spend time with Job during his sickness. Job's current situation was pathetic, to say the least. Job's three friends Eliphaz, Bildad, and Zophar initially acted as true friends as they stayed by his bedside for for quite some time and empathized with him in their silence. In fact, they kept their silence for seven days before they began to give their advice to their friend Job. This journey will try to convince you that extreme suffering is a result of some horrendous sin (or sins). I am just kidding, but these three friends were not. They thought all of the suffering their friend Job had endured was due to an awful sin and that he should repent and seek mercy from God for the mysterious sin.

After all, their friend Job had been labeled as a God-fearing, perfect, and upright man that shunned evil. Now just what did he do to lose his fortune of some ten-thousand head of livestock and his ten children in a single day? Job was the wealthiest man in the east, and his entire lifetime of hard labor was all gone in one day! Just as we fast-forward to the days when Christ was with his disciples, we see a blind man on the scene and his disciples ask the Son of God, "Who sinned? The blind man or his parents?" (John 9). In this case, many thought this man's blindness was a result of some sin committed by himself or his parents. Yet none of them were responsible as his life was displayed so that the works and healing power of God might be made known. It was also appropriate to note that believing in the Son of God can open your eyes to a world never seen just as he did to this blind man in this scripture. We also see those who have wrongly acquired massive fortunes, yet they appear to live the good life and never suffer even until their dying days. As we have already touched on this wisdom, we will tread into perhaps one of the most intriguing stories in the Bible verifying one thing—*do not judge*.

Jesus said, "**Judge not, and ye shall not be judged: condemn not, and ye shall not be condemned: forgive, and ye shall be forgiven**" (Luke 6:37).

The apostle Paul said, "**Let us not therefore judge one another any more: but judge this rather, that no man put a stumbling block or an occasion to fail in his brother's way**" (Romans 14:13).

Paul would most certainly have been a better friend than that of Zophar, but he also urged us not to cause someone to stumble by our actions. If we know some friends are vegetarians, serving them a rib eye dinner wouldn't be wise when you were making them dinner. In the case with Job, there is no mention that Job had done anything wrong. But it seemed everyone thought otherwise and kept prodding Job to repent, for he had to have done something wrong to be covered in painful boils and to have lost everything in such a tragic fashion. No one knew just how many lessons were to be learned as this interaction took place between Job and his friends. No one was aware of the spiritual battle that was taking place right before their eyes. Believe it or not, it all started in heaven.

It may be a shocker for many to know that Satan, being a fallen angel of God, still has access to parts of heaven and is not chained into the pits of hell, at least not yet. We fast-forward to the great tribulation which is soon coming, and we see this happening,

> **"And I heard a loud voice saying in heaven, Now is come salvation, and strength, and the kingdom of our God, and the power of his Christ: for the accuser of our brethren is cast down, which accused them before our God day and night"** (Revelation 12:10).

While there have always been tribulations on this planet since our disobedience in the Garden of Eden, never has there been a time when the full wrath of God, the wrath of Satan, and the wrath of evil men all poured upon the inhabitants of the earth. Never has there been a time like this time to come. While this is an important point to keep in mind, it is not the major point here. The major emphasis in this scripture in Revelation is in one single word—*accuser*. If you are a thief, you are known as a thief, think like a thief, and you act like a thief, then you have no worries of this accuser bothering the heavenly realm with all of your thoughts, actions, and motives. You're not on the accuser's list. You are lost, and he need not accuse you.

There are two lists you need to be aware of that you are either on or you are not. They are different yet similar in many ways. First and foremost is the Book of Life which has recorded the names of the righteous who have placed their faith in God the Father and his Son. The other is the list Satan has to accuse the servants of God. This is perhaps one of the deepest thoughts one might ponder as Satan does not have access to the Book of life, nor can he see the heart of man. Yet he can see the actions of man and hear his voice. He really takes notes when one speaks as he is fully aware of the scripture that says "out of the heart the mouth speaketh." Satan is fully aware of those close to God.

When Satan sees the thief stealing day after day, and he hears his words plotting yet another robbery, he has no need to bother taking his actions to the heavens for debate. He simply continues tempting the thief with more opportunities to continue in his daily routine. Yet, as Satan sees those religious folks, it's fair game, and he puts them on his hit list. Those Christians serving God the most tops his list. At the top of the list is the pastor, then the Sunday school teacher, then the deacons and the choir, and then all those sitting in the pews and watching online. He sets the trap and preys on all of them, striking them hard at their weaknesses. He takes all their misdeeds and mistakes as prizes to heaven as he accuses the brethren night and day. Job had no idea this debate in heaven was taking place.

It is this very scene (back in chapter 1 and 2) where we can see how the accuser was working and still is working against the servants of God. On this day in heaven, God sees Satan and asks him what he has been doing. Satan replies that he has just been his normal self, going between heaven and earth (seeking whom he may devour [1 Peter 5:8]). Then as God already had a plan, he asked Satan if he had ever considered his servant Job as he was an upright man in his eyes. Satan quickly begins accusing Job as he says Job fears God (in reverence) because he has given Job riches and protection. Satan then tells God to take away all that he has, and he will curse him. God then gives Satan permission to take everything of value away from Job, yet he could not touch Job himself. We all know the story as Job then lost his fortune and his children, all in one day, through the work of Satan, which was allowed by God. But Satan did not get his wish as Job rent his clothes in humiliation and prayed to God. He stated that all things come from God, and it was his to give and his to take away. Then he prayed, "Blessed be the name of the Lord." You cannot imagine the disappointment that Satan must have felt when he saw and heard Job's reaction to such a tragic loss. There would come another day when not just an upright and righteous man would have to suffer, but the righteous Savior, the Son of God, would suffer immensely for all of humanity. His name is Jesus Christ and while He was innocent and sinless, He alone provided the atonement man needed to become truly righteous in the eyes of God. Job made sacrifices daily for all of his children. Christ was the sacrifice, and he gave all for all—all those who turn to him.

The scene again goes back into heaven, and the same discussion begins between God and Satan, yet this time, when God brings up his servant Job, Satan now says that if he gets sick enough, he will curse God. God then gives Satan permission to afflict Job but limits him that he cannot take Job's life. Job then suffered immensely as boils covered about all of Job's body. Job's condition was so critical that his wife had even told Job to curse God and die. Yet Job never cursed God throughout all of his pain and losses. The journey we have taken in the twenty-first and twenty-second verses in chapter 20 puts us in the presence of his dear friend, Zophar, giving him advice on how to repent and obtain mercy from God.

Yes, Zophar, was correct as we read early in chapter 20, as he correctly tells how the wicked shall never see the new earth(v. 17), and how the wicked will be judged by all the evil deeds he did in his lifetime (v. 18). His speech also touches on the topic of true substance as the wicked perishes and that which he desired shall be lost forever (v. 20). The journey scripture 20:21–22 shares in the speech that he will have no meat left, thus he has nothing. Back in that day, livestock was like gold. The more livestock you owned, the wealthier you were as Zophar implied Job's loss of livestock robbed him of his wealth.

Guilty. Guilty of being a hypocrite and wicked. This appears to be the general conclusion of Job's three friends. Job's friends, overall, were not bad friends but they were badly mistaken friends who later learned their lessons as the story goes on.

The sad fact is that these three friends are the guilty ones, guilty of falsely judging and jumping to conclusions just as many do today. They were guilty of falling into Satan's role as the accuser and attempting to act as a judge where they had no right to be. Yet Job reveals to his friends just before this speech that he had a Redeemer that took away his guilt by the shedding of innocent blood (19:25). This verse also foretold how his Redeemer would return to the earth in the latter days. The latter days is when the Redeemer will return to the earth and shall stand in the Holy Land. The victory through him is ours for eternity as he is the King of kings and Lord of lords.

These friends of Job had put Job into the pool of trouble and assumed he was now cursed by God. They have now accused him of being unwise, rebellious, and is in great need of mercy from God. He just has to repent this "sinful deed(s)" that he committed. Yet in this story, we must learn we are all in trouble. It is not for us to discern the cause of it. Life is fighting the waves of trouble from childbirth to the grave (Job 5:6–7). Job had the right perspective as he told his friends that everything belongs to God. We are to be good stewards of what God has given us, regardless of how much that is. We have all progressed spiritually and intellectually when we humbly realize that everything belongs to our Creator. God giveth and God taketh away. All of those in eternity can verify that.

It would not be appropriate to end this journey without discussing what happened to these friends of Job. These guys were lucky to be alive as God revealed to them that they were wrong, and they were not speaking the truth (42:7–9). God even tells Eliphaz that his wrath is kindled against him and the other two friends. Can you imagine the fear these friends of Job had when this happened? They quickly obeyed God and made a sacrifice of repentance as God instructed. However, it was not until Job prayed for them that they were cleared from the wrath of God. It almost appears as if Job had to intercede in the midst of the sacrifice for his friends to be forgiven. This could possibly be a glimpse of Christ sitting on the right hand of God, interceding for each of us who have turned to God and trusted in *his sacrifice.*

Also, we could possibly see the prayer of Job for his friends showing that His forgiveness of them opened up more of God's blessings as God restored twice as much as Job had before. Job had difficulty understanding all of this, yet in the end, after realizing the true power and wisdom of God, he repented and ultimately was rewarded abundantly on earth and in heaven. It is a beautiful description of living a lifetime of trouble here on earth as believers and receiving our reward when we meet God.

As we finish the journey in the book of Job, we must be careful not to judge others, my friend.

Now our journey will continue into the Psalms. The twenty-second verse after chapter 20 goes into the following chapter, and it is one of praising and exalting God.

# Chapter 15

## A Journey in the Book of Psalms: Exalt His Name in Praise

**Be thou exalted, LORD, in thine own strength:
So will we sing and praise thy power.**

Many have labeled God incorrectly because as we saw in the journey with Job, that we, as mere humans, just cannot grasp all of who God really is. All that we can do is to pursue him and to know him more intimately by studying and praying. Hopefully, you have a good pastor to lead you in church services, but it is important to spend time in a quiet place with him as you study his Word and pray in your private space. There is possibly no better book in the Bible than the Psalms when one considers the subject of praise and exalting God. We should praise and exalt the Father as he has given an inheritance to His children of a safe dwelling in a quiet place of his own. Planet earth. While many cannot wait to get to heaven, my deepest desire isn't to see the prophets, apostles, friends, family and, yes, our Father and Son in heaven. While I look forward to meeting all of the above, it is my deepest desire to be back here on the new earth with all of those mentioned above. This place is special to me. It is even more special to God. Hey, the Creator put a lot of time into this place! Sure, it will take a lot of work to renovate it, but I'm confident he can accomplish that in his own way. He could very well put us up in the beautiful New Jerusalem hotel while he does this cleansing. There has been healthy debate as to the position of this beautiful city that would stretch nearly the length of the United States and be likewise as high. Does it rest as a pyramid shape and center and rest above Jerusalem? This is the thing we should all dream of, my friend. What a joy it is to put ourselves in this place in the future to come. We need to step out of this world and into eternity as much as we can in our minds and in our thoughts. We need to think upon our real future and seek, praise, and honor the one who made it all possible. The more we accomplish this, the less the world and its problems (which can be very discouraging) can drag us down. Remember the big picture and you will be less anxious about all the sickness, division, chaos, hurt, hatred, and uncertainty that we see today. Peace, joy and happiness are available only through a relationship with God. So go to the river of life and walk into it's waters (Revelation 22:1). The deeper you go, the less strife you will have here on earth. Eat the fruit from the trees by the river. You will then seek to restore relationships and not destroy them. You will hold those harsh thoughts and words to those around you. You will show the love of God in a world filled with hatred. You will have an entirely different perspective when your mind and spirit think about God and spending eternity with him and his family. So go there in your quiet time. Go there when things go wrong. Go there when storms come raging into your life. I assure you that the land promised to you will be there, and it won't be long. Just as the morning sun rises day by day, God assures us all that he will keep his word and deliver his children to our new eternal home, right here on this beautiful planet earth!

**And my people shall dwell in a peaceable habitation, and in sure dwellings, and in quiet resting places;** (Isaiah 32:18)

We are surrounded by prideful and arrogant people in our workplace, in our community and in our governments. These folks in their arrogance are vainly seeking power and the praise of men. We should only praise and exalt the Father, Son and the Holy Spirit.

We must respect those who God has placed as his leaders and pastors, yet they should never be exalted and praised. We will jump a bit into the New Testament as the Bible teaches us that the people in King Herod's day called him god one day, and it was there that Herod exalted himself, and the people praised him, and that very day, God took Herod's life.

King Herod had just killed the apostle James, the brother of John, and as that pleased the Jews, he sought out Peter and planned to kill him as well. Peter was imprisoned by Herod and was going to put him on trial after Passover. Yet, the church prayed without ceasing for Peter, and an angel of God came to the jail and freed Peter the night before he was to appear before Herod. Herod was furious and had the jail keepers all killed. One day, Herod gave a speech to the people, and they were amazed and called him a god. Just as he was accepting the praise and loving it, an angel of God smote King Herod, and he died and he was eaten by worms. This was a horrible way to die. There were two major issues here, and the issues were that both Herod and the people chose to praise and exalt man and not God.

> **According to their pasture, so were they filled; they were filled, and their heart was exalted; therefore have they forgotten me.** (Hosea 13:6)

> **For whosoever exalted himself shall be abased; and he that humbleth himself shall be exalted.** (Luke 14:11)

Herod failed in all of his glory to give God the glory and to exalt the source and provider of his position of power. The result was not just death; the worms ate his flesh in front of all to see. What a horrid way to die for Herod, the Roman ruler over Judaea. While this was one event and one king to be remembered for exalting himself, we must also remember another one that will exalt himself in the last days found in the book of Daniel. Perhaps one of the most noted spiritual battles among angels is brought to light here. Daniel was a true servant of God as he yearned to know God and his plans for Israel. He prayed and fasted for Israel daily, and in this case, he had prayed and fasted for twenty-one days. God had sent his angel Gabriel to Daniel to reveal the future of Israel and the world governments. We haven't the time in this book to discuss the precious and valuable truths of the book of Daniel, so you should study this book as much as you can when you have time. It should be no surprise this book is remarkably accurate in describing the kingdoms that reigned the earth from Daniel's time to the latter days that have yet to come.

The angel, Gabriel, was sent to Daniel to deliver God's message but was held up fighting for twenty days with the prince of Persia. The arch angel, Michael, came to help Gabriel to defeat these evil angels and allow Gabriel to continue on his journey to Daniel. Why was there such a great spiritual battle to prevent this explanation to be revealed? Fate. The fate of the one great deceiver is revealed in this revelation during the last days. Satan's desire to be exalted and praised will be fulfilled, and though it is just for a brief moment, there will be those—believe it or not—that have followed him and will worship him. Satan will persecute and kill those who oppose him with great wrath. This will occur during the time of the great tribulation. Satan will desecrate the temple built in Jerusalem. He will desecrate the temple which will be rebuilt in Jerusalem and break the covenant (agreement or peace plan) between Israel and the Palestinians. He will not only claim to be god, but he will speak things against the Lord of Hosts. Many scholars feel the new temple construction will begin at or around the time of the departure of the bride (the rapture). These scholars estimate the time to construct the temple to be three and a half years, and they could be correct in this estimation. The Antichrist will exalt himself in the newly constructed temple that will exist during the tribulation period.

> **And the king shall do according to his will; and he shall exalt himself, and magnify himself above every god.** (Daniel 11:36)

Yet after he makes great strides in securing and taking parts of the Holy Land, the dragon (Satan), the beast (antichrist), and the false prophet face a major obstacle in their conquest for power.

> **And he shall plant the tabernacles of his palace between the seas in the glorious holy mountain; yet <u>he shall come to his end</u>, and none shall help him.** (Daniel 11:45)

The great deceiver's fate has been revealed to a prophet, and Satan's prince of Persia tried but failed to stop this from being known. When the desecration of the temple takes place, the true evil nature of the beast will be revealed to the people of Israel as well as the rest of the world. The Jewish people must flee to the mountains of safety just as they did in AD 70 when the Romans destroyed the temple. Many scholars feel they may flee to Petra for safety. This will be a disturbing and terrible time for the world and the Jewish nation. Even though many will be martyred during this time, the majority of people on earth will be rebellious and follow the deceiver. They will also be forever destined to the fate of the great deceiver as well.

David did fail in many ways, and he failed big-time. As discussed earlier, David struggled in the flesh as he was guilty of adultery, murder, and other sins in his life. Yet God could see his heart, and he begged for forgiveness and got up and pursued God. He loved God. He exalted God. He praised God. Now if you wonder what it takes to be a man or woman after God's own heart, it does not involve how many times you went to church; it doesn't matter how much money you put in the offering plate, nor how much work you have done for God. If you want to have a soul after God's own heart, you must accept Him for who He really is and not a fabrication of what you want Him to be. You must love and adore him. You must see just how miserable you are and how deep in trouble you are in. You must see his hand for your rescue and grab hold of it. If you read the psalms of David, you will see that he had been rescued numerous times, and he knew the source of his protection. He was thankful for all things, all protections, all rewards, and all his redemption provided by the Father of Abraham, Isaac, and Jacob. David exalted and praised God.

We must exalt and praise him for he inhabits the praise of those that love him! For he is worthy to be praised.

# Chapter 16

## A Journey in the Book of Proverbs: The Substance of Your Inheritance

**An Inheritance may be gotten hastily at the beginning: but the end thereof shall not be blessed. Say not thou, I will recompense evil; but wait on the LORD, and He shall save thee.**

Many are fortunate to get an inheritance from a family member, and some individuals become instantly wealthy upon receiving their inheritance. If you recall the opening sermon on Thomas Mountain, you will recall the recognition of those in eternity describing what true substance really is. While there are major differences of opinion in defining true value between those saved and those not, none could realize a true inheritance like those in eternity.

Inheritance involves at least a party of two. One being the person that gives, and the other being the person who receives. The giver must have something of value to give or the person receiving the gift would not consider it actually being an inheritance. Also, the person giving the gift has favored the person that is now placed in their will. Usually there is a legal will made who identifies the giver as well as the receiver of the possessions to be given.

Do you have a will? Or better yet, do you have someone that you would be willing to give all of your possessions to should you pass away? Do you anticipate receiving an inheritance from a relative? All of these questions are driven by our determination of just what we have to give and what we would hope to receive. Many folks get an inheritance, and they invest it wisely so that not only do they benefit, but benefits their family as well. This journey is focusing on an inheritance that is gotten hastily, and there is "no blessing" associated with it. The scripture also instructs us to allow God to deal with those being unjust to us as we live here on earth. God will deal with our enemies, and we must trust Him to do so. So let's now consider the term *inheritance* as we continue on. How many times have you heard of someone blowing their inheritance? We are all guilty of making remarks about those who are born with silver spoons in their mouths as they inherited a vast amount of wealth and they never had to work for anything.

There is a story in Luke 15 that Jesus told of a young son prematurely asking his father for his share of his inheritance. This son thought the grass was truly greener on the other side of the meadow as he took his inheritance and travelled away from home, enjoying the high life with wild women and wild parties. I am sure this guy had a lot of friends until the money ran out! Then trouble came into the land with a famine, and the son found himself starving to death and eating with the pigs. He finally realized the huge mistake he had made as he realized even the servants of his father had good food to eat. He then repented and decided to journey back home and seek forgiveness from his father.

Home was the safe place he had foolishly abandoned, and now he realized the value and security of a loving father. Many family members would not welcome someone like this prodigal son home. Yet his father saw him far off as he was coming home, and when he saw his son, he was filled with compassion and ran to meet his son. He grabbed his son with a loving hug and kissed him. The son repents to his father, and then the father responds immediately by ordering a robe for his son and for his servants to prepare the best of his cattle for a feast! What joy this young lad had to have experienced to get such a welcoming from his father! There is no better picture that describes our heavenly Father and his love for you and me. God loves us unconditionally regardless of our failures and is willing to forgive any who truly repent and turn away from the pig pen they have laid in. The fine white linen is not given to all, but to all who persevere in faithfulness in their devotion to Christ.

This story takes a bad turn momentarily as the older son is less than thrilled to see his brother return in rags after he blew all of his inheritance. He asks his father, "Why are you preparing such a feast for a son who deserted all of us for a brief thrill?" The father then assures the elder son of his inheritance but said they must celebrate and be glad because his brother was lost, and now he is found.

We clearly see that Jesus is telling the story that reflects his Father who has given liberally to all of mankind. Yet most squander it and never consider the work, the love, and the care it took to acquire it. If you take a man who has labored in the field day after day, then he will have a completely different perspective of wealth from someone who has inherited the same wealth. He spends his money wisely as it took a lot of blood, sweat, and tears to attain it. I mean, seriously, did you make the trees that built your home? Did you stir up a batter that seeded the earth for the cattle to graze upon? Did you speak, and the water just began to pour out of your faucet? Absolutely not, nor did you put that money in the bank on your own. Everything you possess is a gift from God, and while they may be enjoyed, these gifts shouldn't be worshipped. The love of money is the root of all—well, you know the rest of the sentence. There are two reasons for gold and silver: One is for us to enjoy. God wants us to enjoy the fruits of our hard labor. The second is to test the hearts of men. Take a quick look at your checkbook, and then tell me how much you really love the Father. I am not asking for an offering either. Any profit that may be made from this book will *all* be used to further the kingdom of God, not my savings account. This book is not about me nor is it to secure my retirement account. It is about God and his inheritance that he gives to those who seek and love him.

Evil is more than just Satan running to and fro, accusing the brethren and deceiving the world. It consists of principalities and rulers of darkness in high places. It consists of a spirit of rebellion toward a sovereign God and it has a snowball effect from there. Evil simply forgoes God being Lord of your life, to *you* being lord of your life. Evil involves multitudes, feeding not only on Satan's bible of deception, but they are feeding their minds with a self-centered bible which rivals God's Holy Word. Evil has taken its toll on our educational systems of the world, the governmental systems of the world, the traditional families of the world and the truths of the Gospel and messages from the Bible. Evil would also like to eliminate the word *inheritance* from the Bible as all of those following Satan have an inheritance of misery and suffering in the eternal Lake of Fire. That's not much to look forward to for all those associated with Satan:

**For evildoers shall be cut off: but those that wait upon the Lord, they shall inherit the earth.** (Psalm 25:13)

Satan deeply resents those that have an inheritance that is laid up in store for them in heaven. It's the desire of Satan and his followers to rob mankind of this inheritance that is simply not possible for them to attain. Mankind follows the same evil pattern. Always remember that the law of God results in death, which is the second death for that person refusing the sacrifice of Christ. The soul who has accepted Jesus Christ as their Lord and Savior has the indwelling of the Holy Spirit in their soul. While the soul is tempted, it is directed and comforted by the Spirit of God, which dwells within. This indwelling always has its confrontations of the human flesh as the flesh is weak in all of us. Yet the Spirit is a blessing and a gift from God, and as the faithful are resting in the work and righteousness of Christ, the unfaithful are subject to the law and judgment of the Father.

The inheritance of both the faithful and the unfaithful is established and recorded in real time, and should you die now, your inheritance is set. It will first be revealed when you are taken away by the angels, and second in the judgments of God. The faithful will be rewarded in the judgment seat of Christ and will be rewarded by the good deeds we did while on earth. The unfaithful will remain in the pit of darkness until the Great White Throne Judgment and all the souls that chose to follow evil will be judged on every single act of disobedience that they committed in adulthood. This very scene should shake some to their core. It should awaken some to realize the billions of dollars of wealth on earth has absolutely no value in this judgment. The bribing done on earth will no longer work in the great white throne judgment.

Considering all of this should give us all a better perspective on who has what on this earth as we live. While some on earth have more than others, it is up to God to number the blessings one has, regardless of how we feel about it. There are those who have hoarded to the highest heavens, yet they still hoard more and more. Yet others may be blessed by working for that wealthy person and have made a living as a result of his success. Other unfaithful people have may have invented something that has provided a means to share the Gospel of Christ throughout the world. Hitler's Holocaust had a result that he never would have desired as the United Nations voted to re-establish Israel as a nation while being sympathetic to his evil intent. We often never realize how things will eventually work out until after the fact. One of my favorite scriptures is Romans 8:28, **"And we know that all things work together for good to them that love God, to them who are the called according to his purpose."**

True, faithful and mature Christians seek God, not other's faults and failures. Those who have done well in life, regardless of their position with God, is a matter between God and them, not anyone else. We must bathe ourselves in the love of God. We can only imagine the beautiful new earth and the inheritance God has so graciously has in store for us. We simply just can't imagine. Those who have chosen the reward of the world will also have no idea of the degree of loneliness, despair, suffering, and anguish that awaits them forever. It is their reward and inheritance. Evil never reveals this to the unfaithful soul as the poor soul is fed by the desires of the world. This is because the great deceiver dreadfully awaits the same fate and the same reward. While the wealth of the unfaithful will soon vanish, the Word and truth of God shall last forever. Rewards again are given to both the faithful and the unfaithful. I can safely say that many on earth who were poor, according the standards of society, will be rich in the new heavens and the new earth. We should help the poor and let the rich know that their wealth is from God and God only. We therefore must challenge the unfaithful rich to realize the source of their wealth and to pray for their salvation. The Bible makes it very clear that you cannot serve God and money. There is nothing wrong with having money. It is all wrong when money has you.

Everyone has an inheritance on earth as well as in eternity. Again, we should not judge anyone by what they have, regardless of their worth. The Bible makes it very clear that the first on earth shall be last, and the last shall be first. This biblical reference surely tells us not to foolishly attempt to evaluate one's assets. That should be left to God and God alone.

We know from the book of Exodus that Israel shall inherit the land that God promised them. From this early time in Israel's history until now, we can see this is still a "work in process."

**By little and little I will drive them out from before thee, until thou be increased, and inherit the land.** (Exodus 33:30)

Those who argue that others should share this land with Israel as well as those who think Israel should be wiped off the map should go back and read this chapter in Exodus. God promised this land to Israel for an everlasting dwelling place, and while the earth will be renewed in ways we cannot imagine, Israel will still remain. The Mount of Olives will split in two when the Son of God returns and will sit on the throne in his everlasting kingdom. This is the moment both God and the faithful have been looking forward to. What a great time to be on this planet! Always remember, the land belongs to the Jews because their Father (and our Father) promised them the land as part of their inheritance.

**Thy people also shall be all righteous: they shall inherit the land for ever, the branch of my planting, the work of my hands, that I may be glorified**. (Isaiah 60:21)

To really inherit something, it must have substance and only God can deliver true substance. All you have to do is to love him and then love others.

> **That I may cause those that love me to inherit substance; and I will fill their treasures.**
> (Proverbs 8:21)

*Go right, not left.*
I am not speaking about any political party here, as I am speaking on your position right here, right now should you pass on to eternity (Matthew 25:34).

> **Then shall the King say unto them on his right hand, Come, ye blessed of my Father, inherit the kingdom prepared for you from the foundation of the world.**

Got substance?

# CHAPTER 17

## A Journey in the Book of Isaiah: Babylon and Arabia

> **The burden upon Arabia. In the forest in Arabia shall ye lodge, O ye travelling companies of Dedanim. The inhabitants of the land of Tema brought water to him that was thirsty, they prevented with their bread him that fled.**

This journey could very well take another book to complete as the twenty-first and twenty-second verses go into the following chapter. God is discussing the fate of both Babylon and mentions the city of Dedan in the forest of Arabia. Those mentioned of Dedan have descendants now dwelling in Saudi Arabia. The movement of these descendants of Ishmael back then involved a lot of war and fighting as mentioned here. The scripture mentions in the verses leading to the burden of Arabia, the fall of Babylon.

To understand the descendants of Ishmael and the burden of such peoples and his descendants, requires a further and deeper study into Islam. Islam and Babylon are both topics that could take a book to describe their roles in the latter days. The problem with both Islam and the Babylonian Empire is that neither places the Son of God in his true being. Always remember that the three persons—God the Father, God the Son, and God the Holy Sprit—are all separate and personal. This trinity offers internal healing to those who are hurting. This trinity gives understanding to those who are confused. This trinity gives peace to those who are fearful. This trinity gives hope to those who feel helpless. This trinity gives strength to those who are weary. They work in unity as the finished work of Jesus Christ personally made this all possible to those who believe, trust, and follow Him. The dividing line in all religions is made by who Jesus is, what he did, and what he is going to do. We will not go into any religion bashing but rather point to the one true way to heaven, and that is through Jesus Christ. He and he alone is the Savior of the world. We need to pray for all those in other religions to know who Jesus is and that he can and will deliver them.

Those in Arabia (now Saudi Arabia) have been blessed by God as he promised. Ishmael was a descendant of Abraham, not chosen by God but by Sarah. Sarah and Abraham were weary of waiting on God to have a son. Sarah offered her maid Hagar to Abraham to have the child Ishmael. This was the plan of man and not the plan of God. Many from the Islamic world have had their eyes opened and taken the narrow gate that few take to Christianity.

While not all Islamic folks are radical, evil terrorists, they must realize their religion is not based on the truth of Christ and who he really is. There is no question that many will be deceived (especially early on) during the tribulation in the latter days, but as persecution increases toward those who refuse the authority and the mark of the beast, many eyes will be opened, and hearts will be changed. Many people with Christian backgrounds as well as of other religions won't accept the mark (quite possibly a chip) during the tribulation and choose to be faithful to Christ. These committed individuals will be severely persecuted and martyred as they will be blamed for all the calamity and chaos that takes the world by storm.

The antichrist will make war with those that have a testimony for Jesus Christ. Through him, the beast and the false prophet, an attempt is made to imitate the triune of God. There will be many faiths of those who were not truly in God's family and not even thinking of him that will fall into Satan's trap of deception. Strong delusion will engulf the minds of most during this horrendous time of judgment. You do not want to wait until this time to make things right with God.

The hope of the faithful church is that just as the days of Noah and Sodom and Gomorrah were, so are the days going to be just before the tribulation begins. The Bible teaches the faithful shall be taken to safety, just as God provided safety to Noah and his family. Christ assures us that two shall be standing at the mill, and one will be taken and the other left. Two shall also be in bed, and one will be taken and the other left. This is again the departure or catching up of those faithful Christians who are watching and waiting for his return. We should live our lives as if we were going to live to the age of one hundred, yet we need to live each day in great anticipation for the Lord to come. It is crucial that one is not confused by "only those watching and waiting for the Lord" will be taken in the rapture. I, nor anyone else, can identify the position of another in the eyes of God. I am by no means implying work has to be done to go to glory. Yet in the book of Revelation, Christ is speaking to the churches in AD 95 as well as to the churches today. We have loosely and falsely identified "Christians" in today's society by our own impressions and not of God's specific requirements. Again, we erroneously judge and cannot see the intentions of the heart of anyone. Watching is not just merely looking to the sky for the glory cloud and waiting on your porch for the Lord. It is a state of mind—a state of faith that one is living. If you do not think this status of faith can vary, then the words *watch*, *ready*, and *prepared* Christ used would all have to be removed from the scriptures. Anyone who thinks everyone is rewarded the same is kidding himself, especially when you consider all that Christ said to the seven churches. It would take another book for this to be really explained in depth. One thing is certain, and that is all those who are taken in the departure will be faithful. They will be ready. They will be watching. They will be prepared. They will be living in the light of the Lord. They will have fruit on their limbs. True Christians bear fruit only because Christ is the vine. Perseverance has its rewards.

> I am the vine, ye are the branches: He that
> abideth in me, and I in him, the same bringeth

forth much fruit: for without me ye can do nothing. (John 15:5)

We, as humans, are the branches and will produce fruit only if we are in the family of God. This book is not for the reader to become a fruit evaluator of others but to seriously evaluate the fruit that *your* life has produced and is currently producing. Only God sees the inner heart of man as well as his degree of faithfulness to him. Yet I am led to challenge those who say they are Christians as well as those "almost persuaded" to carefully evaluate your heart and true motives. It is impossible to work your way into heaven and to be given the gift of eternal life. Yet it is impossible to be in the vine of Christ and not produce some level of fruit. One needs to live the life of a faithful servant as described by Christ. One of the faithful's rewards is to ride behind him as he returns to earth in all his glory. Again, the scriptures are clear that the called, the chosen, and the faithful will be following him to the earth in great power and glory (Revelation 17 and 19). One might then ask the question, "Is the rapture a right, or is it a reward?" This question is not a concern for those living a faithful life to the Lord. This has nothing to do with the works of a servant and has everything to do with the servant's faithfulness. There also should be discernment between the words *unfaithful* (faithless) and *unfaithful servants*. Again one might ask how much faith must one have to be taken in the rapture? *Enough faith to watch*. One might then assume this thought would eliminate those fine Christians who support the mid and post-tribulation return of Christ. This absolutely does not as if you seriously consider what Christ has said concerning his return for his bride. If you're watching as the good servant was and if you have kept oil for the long night waiting on the Groom and if you have kept his word as those in the church of Philadelphia did and you have the faith and anticipation that he is coming, then you are the called, the chosen, and the *faithful*. It really doesn't matter if you believe he is coming before, after, or in the middle of the tribulation as long as you are watching and waiting for his return. Every true believer living should be doing just that. Again, I will say this topic should not be one that the brethren fight and argue over. If you are ready, it shouldn't be an issue. With these thoughts in mind, let's consider the Christians spoken of who are persecuted during the tribulation that are martyred. One must consider carefully *who* these martyrs might be.

Could they possibly be:

- the unfaithful servants? (Matthew 25:30)
- the unwise virgins? (Matthew 25:11–12)
- The servants who think His coming is delayed? (Matthew 24:48–50)
- those with spotted garments? (Revelation 3:4, 7:14)
- those letting thorns rule their lives? (Luke 8:14, Matthew 13:22)
- some members in the church pew like the church of Sardis? (Revelation 3:3)
- some members in the church pew like the church of Laodicea? (Revelation 3:14–22)
- some members in the church pew like the church of Ephesus? (Revelation 2:4)
- some members in the church pew like the church of Pergamos? (Revelation 2:14)
- some members in the church pew like the church of Thyatira? (Revelation 2:20)

Wow, not many folks teach and preach on these souls that will be persecuted, beaten, tortured, and martyred during the tribulation. Yet, they just might include those listed above. If you qualify to be on the list above, I would greatly encourage you to join the list below.

- One in the Church pew of Philadelphia—Revelation 3:7
- One who loves his appearing—2 Timothy 4:8
- One of the wise virgins—Matthew 25:10
- One of the faithful servants—25:23
- One who has kept his word—Revelation 3:10
- One who is faithful—Revelation 17:14

- One who is producing fruit—John 15:5
- One in the book of remembrance—Malachi 3:16–18
- One with Christ as he opens the seals of the tribulation—Revelation 5:9-10

One might consider the tribulation's wrath from God is directed to those who are his enemy and to those who willfully worship the beast (antichrist) as his anger (the cup of wrath) reaches his limit. Many servants are martyred and persecuted during this time as God's wrath and judgment is being poured upon the wicked (Jeremiah 30:23–24). These wicked men will be shaking their fists at God instead of giving Him their hearts! You have to remember as the rapture and tribulation will first shock the multitudes, hearts will become harder for many, yet during this time, many eyes will now be opened and hearts changed as the seven years progress. Christ comes as a thief in which he takes something of great value and is then gone in the night. I cannot wait to be stolen!

One might also consider the chastisement Christ was speaking of when addressing the Laodicean church (Revelation 3:19). These folks have gotten comfortable in playing church and have forgotten Christ. They have been blinded by the world and put value on earthly things that erode their relationship with Christ. Christ calls the Church of Laodicea lukewarm, and He says he "will spue thee out of my mouth (Revelation 3:16). They might just land right in the persecution days of the tribulation. Christ makes it clear that those who overcome will sit with him and the Father on the throne. Please notice this was the last church that he addressed and many scholars feel this could be the church atmosphere of today. The lukewarm church. Again, all true believers are free from the eternal wrath God has placed on those without faith in him. However, we see through the ages he has disciplined (chastised) the Jewish nation due to their disobedience and rebellion. There is a direct parallel defined by Christ in considering the churches Jesus addresses in Revelation. He is now bringing up chastisement to the disobedient in many of the churches. He said the *overcomers* would sit with him on the throne and one could rightly assume we are with him as he opens the seals of the tribulation which comes in the next chapters. We should also consider those being tormented by the plagues and judgments to the wicked during the tribulation. The persecution of those refusing the mark will come at a cost to those faithful to Satan and his kingdom. God's wrath intensifies as those following him are being persecuted by Satan's empire. His word clearly states his wrath was upon those who took the mark of the beast and *worshipped* his image. This plague is revealed which describes the sores that God places on all those receiving the mark of the beast in chapter 16, verse 2. While some do not take the mark and while they are under severe persecution, they are spared from this terrible disease. The environment during the tribulation will be horrific, to say the least. But regardless of one's beliefs, there will be those making commitments to Christ during the tribulation and this number will include more than the twelve tribes of Israel. Many label those left behind as backsliders, and some even say they are those claiming to be Christians who never truly committed their lives to the Lord Jesus. I won't go there in defining who these souls are. I will not define those truly saved and those who are not. I won't define those who are worthy. I won't define the faithful and the unfaithful. I won't define those knocking on the door after it is closed by the Bridegroom. I will not define those who Christ chastises for being lukewarm and has lost their love for him. I am absolutely not qualified to do such a thing nor would I want to try. No one on this earth is qualified. Yet the scriptures are clear that these kinds of individuals will exist during the last days. It is, however, the objective of this book for everyone reading to again evaluate your true position with God. Too many label themselves as "Christians" and many have fabricated a culture that you are "Christian" if you merely claim it, attend some Christian function, or have simply just been raised by Christian parents. While being truly saved does, in fact, deliver us from the eternal wrath of God we are all born into, we must not be blinded and drift away from Him during our life. So one could assume that the five unwise virgins Christ spoke of did go into tribulation due to their unpreparedness and letting the cares of the world rule their lives. They just forgot all that Christ had done for them. They thought they were going to the wedding, yet the door was shut. Again, studying the seven Churches in Revelation, we see Christ addressing *the church* and their shortfalls. So when the door was shut and they were experiencing the tribulation, these unwise virgins are not direct targets of God's wrath but the targets of Satan and evil men. The tribulation is a time of great darkness upon the earth. While many agree this time of darkness of hatred, division, and confusion has already begun, it gets much worse once the true bride of Christ is called to heaven. The great deception (or the great tribulation) will then be led by Satan as those multitudes turning to God will be attacked by those loyal to Satan and the antichrist. The wrath of God will be upon those serving Satan, yet many followers of God and Christ will suffer immensely from the wrath of Satan. As the wrath increases on the wicked, the persecution is increased to those who have the testimony of Jesus Christ and keep the commandments of God (Revelation 12:17).

There are plenty of examples of those both in the Old and New Testaments who are faithless as well as some unfaithful *servants*. Be aware of the difference. It is the writer in Hebrews:

**"And unto them that look for him shall he appear the second time"** (Hebrews 9:28).

The scriptures tell us that God is a rewarder of those who *diligently* seek him. Many may argue that this thought may allow for the teaching of an erroneous or partial loss of your salvation, which may confuse those reading this book.

It is clear that once you confess the Lord Jesus as Lord and Savior and you believe in your heart that Christ rose from the dead, then you are not only saved but also sealed with the Holy Spirit of God. You are in the family of God. While the degree of fruit produced may vary among the family of God, all those truly saved will have some degree of fruit. One example in scripture is Christ being the sower and mankind being the seed (Matthew 13) throughout the world (field). It should be noted that the tares in this parable were clearly those who produced no fruit whatsoever. They were deceived by the wicked one and will all be cast into hell. Please take note of those who were overtaken by the cares of this world and choked out and became "unfruitful." Many could argue that these folks could be compared to the unfruitful of the Jews as they became unfaithful before the Father. Once more, I simply want to encourage all who are reading to simply draw nigh to God. Then this debate and discussion will go to the wayside. Live your life, and cherish each day with your loved ones and friends. Yet as you draw nigh to God, he will draw others nigh to you as they see something in your life that they desperately need, fruit—fruit that is a result of your peace, joy, and love that comes from the Holy Spirit of God.

> **When you are in the vine and you are of the good seed then some will produce a hundredfold, some sixty and yet some thirty.** (Matthew 13:23)

Christ sees how much time and materials we truly devote to Him just as He saw the widowed woman that gave 2 mites into the temple treasury. She was poor. She was possibly neglected in her society. Yet she was greatly esteemed by Jesus as he saw her faithfulness. She had given all that she had even though it was only a small amount. Be careful not to judge others. I encourage all of you to not be a tare and not to be those who become unfruitful (unfaithful). Let the love of God be reflected in your life. For great is your reward. The alternative is to be disciplined or chastised by Jesus. Our reward awaits us, and it is not just a great reward but a reward of true substance and of one we cannot comprehend.

Remember the rewards you get depend upon your work and dedication to the kingdom of God. Paul clearly states in 1 Thessalonians that we are to be sober and watching and living in the light of our Lord Jesus. Jesus also clearly states in Revelation that there will be rewards for some in the church and chastisement for others.

> **And that servant, which knew his lords' will, and prepared not himself, neither did according to his will, shall be beaten with many stripes.** (Luke 12:47)

A careful study of the seven churches will certainly give you a better understanding of all the flaws we see in the church atmosphere then and today. The Bible has a message for mankind through eternity and not just for some in a particular time and place. So consider the multitude under the alter (Revelation 7) during the place in time of Revelation 17. It is very doubtful this great multitude who John sees are new converts. There is a way that seems right in the eyes of man that actually leads him through a path of chastisement. When the departure of the faithful happens, multitudes will understand what has happened, and though they realize the door is shut to the wedding, they realize they can make it to the festival. They will be there as friends of the Groom. Many have said the Jews will be considered the guests during this great celebration that will continue as Christ returns to earth. Most of the folks refusing the mark of the beast will be killed for their faith in Christ. Some may call this group the unsaved, backsliders, the ones who lost their first love for Christ, the unfaithful servants, the unprepared virgins, etc.; yet I will simply call them "those in **Revelation 7:14.**"

**These are they that came out of the great tribulation, and have washed their robes, and made them white in the blood of the Lamb.**

It again should be noted that *after* the triumphal entry of Christ and his faithful, these souls are brought to the earth as noted in Revelation 20:4–6 for the millennial reign of Christ. They were *not* present at the marriage supper of the Lamb nor given the fine white linen as described in Revelation 19.

So labeling these martyred souls is something I refuse to do and neither should you, though if you could possibly be one of those possible candidates, I encourage you to get oil in your lamp as the Holy Spirit needs to be welcomed and living with joy in your heart. We should not quench the Spirit sent to comfort us. You may dispute all of this if you wish as it is a difficult and unpopular topic to many. Yet this message will make sense to many who are merely pretending to be in the family of God. It will make sense to those living the life as those disobedient church members in the five churches Jesus addresses in his revelation to John. He does not find fault in two of the churches. Examine yourself, and be honest with yourself. Have you forgotten and neglected the Bridegroom? Are you actually producing fruit? Now consider for a moment the huge multitude of souls under the altar in heaven (Revelation 7:14).

These souls now wear their white robes (stained by cares of this world?) that were cleansed by the blood of the Lamb. I again will not judge anyone, though I will warn those living life as those in the church of Sardis, stained with the sins of their lifestyle. Also, consider those in the church of Pergamos and Thyatira as as they were living a lifestyle that casts them into "great tribulation" (Revelation 2:22).

One must consider that these words came to the apostle John as one of the last messages given in the entire Bible. We must all take heed to the message Jesus gives us concerning the church. To whom much is given, much is required (Luke 12). Addressing the church is the first thing Jesus does before describing the upcoming judgments. Christ reveals so many things that will happen so that we, like the church of Philadelphia, will know that our faithfulness and the keeping His Word in our hearts and our lifestyle will be rewarded. He assures this church they will be accounted worthy to escape the time that tries the entire world. (Revelation 3:7–11) While our salvation is eternally secured, the consequence of unfaithfulness is chastisement. If one chooses to live a life out of the will of God, then he will allow you, but beware of the consequences.

### As many as I love, I rebuke and chasten: be zealous therefore, and repent. (Revelation 3:19)

There is a definite pattern in the Old Testament, as we consider the Jews who became unfaithful and let their faith waiver to the point they strayed deeply into the darkness of idolatry. Did the entire nation then go to hell? I would think not, yet save for Joshua and Caleb, none were allowed to enter the promised land. One also might consider the five virgins that ran out of oil that Jesus spoke of. Did they go to hell after failing to get to the wedding due to their lack of preparedness? I would not think so. They may have missed the wedding itself, but they could very well have gone to the festival as guests. Remember, the wedding party consists of the bride, the groom, the guests, and the friends of the groom. While the wedding and the marriage supper of the Lamb are in heaven, the celebration will continue and move to the earth during Christ's millennial reign. I encourage you to rid your life of idols and obstacles that dominate your life. I encourage you to strive to get *intimate* with the Groom and yearn for that wedding day. Christ will close the door as this great supper is held exclusively for the faithful bride and the groom. *This* will be intimacy at its greatest height.

As we tread into the deeper waters of our relationship with Christ, we may still sin, but we strive *not* to. The unfaithful Jews were most certainly chastised by the Father, as we read in the books of Hosea and Lamentations. It should not be ignored that those unfaithful to His Son would likewise be chastened. I would encourage each reader to keep the Word of God as you can hear his voice every time you read the Bible. If you are one of those living the life of those in the church of Philadelphia, then you should not be concerned for yourself as you have overcome the cares of this world and kept his Word. However, if you are one of those *not* living the life of those of Philadelphia church but one of the unprepared virgins, then I would hate to see your crown taken away. It may be a shock to those knowing that you can have a crown awarded to you yet later taken away (Revelation 3:11). While the weight of salvation is constant and on the shoulders of our Redeemer, the weight of our faithfulness varies with each believer. Therefore, let us all increase our faith by diligently studying, meditating, praying, and serving our beloved Savior. By doing so, he promised that those being worthy would certainly escape the tribulation to come.

> **And take heed to yourselves, lest at any time your hearts be overcharged with surfeiting, and drunkenness, and cares of this life, and so that day come upon you unawares.**

> **For as a snare shall it come on all them that dwell on the face of the whole earth. Watch ye therefore, and pray always, that ye may be accounted worthy to escape all these things that shall come to pass, and to stand before the Son of man.** (Luke 21:34–36)

Take a moment and listen to the "Midnight Cry" by Ivan Parker.

This book is not to confuse but to encourage and to move us all closer to God and his Son. The topic and timing of the rapture are heavily debated as we are nearing the latter days. It is good to have a healthy debate, but I refuse to argue with any of my brothers and sisters concerning this great event. So we will sum it up by simply saying to be faithful enough to watch, my friend, and to look forward to his appearing. That's what is really important. Be saved, be looking, and be ready. How hard is that?

Now we will return to the Middle East as Arabia and Babylon are definitely featured in the latter days. As we examine the fighting atmosphere in this journey, we notice those in Arabia being mentioned. Don't think for a moment that all Arabic people will forget God, as we see in the book of Ezekiel (chapter 38) where Saudi Arabia is challenging the forces of Russia, Turkey, and Iran as these countries are invading Israel. Given the current state of affairs in the world today, it should be no surprise this invasion could occur. Today we see some Arabic countries finding favor with Israel with Saudi Arabia appearing to be leading the way as they oppose Iran's ambitions. There will be a day coming when Russia, Turkey, and Iran threaten Israel, and it is amazing the Ezekiel 38 prophecy foretells how Saudi Arabia questions this action along with the "young lions" (possibly the US and Britain).

How long ago was the book of Ezekiel written? I thought I would add a little food for thought for those still looking to disprove God. We now see these nations are unified just as prophesied in Ezekiel 38.

Make no mistake about it, while God has shown himself in so many ways to all of us, he, because of his nature, must make the final call to cleanse the heavens and the earth. This cleansing unfortunately, will catch most folks off guard as the worldly system (Babylonian influence) has slowly and methodically taken the hearts and souls of man deep into the sea of darkness. Little light is left as man is sinking near the depths of no return. The Bible makes it clear during the times of the Great Tribulation that man "repented not" of their sin, still clinging to the lust of the world and its short-lived pleasures. The darkness will get even darker. Those living just prior to the flood in Noah's day, those living in Lot's day in Sodom, those living in Pompeii just prior to the eruption all had one thing in common—most of them had been blinded so badly that the only time they could clearly see their fate was when they opened their eyes in the total darkness of the pit. It was then too late. They had all allowed their hearts and souls to be hardened, and all the warnings and calls from God's servants never had any effect on them. This was such a horrible fate for each of these souls, and take heed that your fate does not end likewise. Remember, every adult gets a second—a second death or a second life. Both are an eternal place of consciousness and physical presence. Most souls on earth are sentenced to a second death, or simply an eternal separation from God who casts them into the lake of fire (Revelation 20:15). I plead for those readers who are currently included in this great number to be born again. This second birth is a birth into everlasting life and to an inheritance unspeakable and indescribable. While these journeys all present interesting stories, all of the Bible pleads for the restoration of the relationship between God and yourself. The lost souls in hell from Sodom, the flood, and Pompeii all had their chance; however, their eternal lives came at a time they never expected.

Things on earth moved from normal to extremely dire very quickly. Judgment comes with the speed of race horses. Those from Sodom, the days of the flood, and Pompeii could tell you that. These souls will tell you from the pit of darkness not to fall prey to their fate and to seek the way, the truth, and the life in Jesus Christ. (John 14:6)

God has shown us throughout history two huge characteristics that he possesses: *One*, his unwavering love, grace, and mercy to all of humanity. *Two*, his wrath and judgment to all those who refuse his love, grace, and mercy.

To all of those who dispute these characteristics, you may think otherwise. The weight, the magnitude, and the essence of his love is also balanced by his wrath and judgment. God is God. Some take Him, some ignore Him, but all will meet Him in judgment. God never changes. Many fail to realize the wrath and judgment side of God. He has not hidden this side of him, as so many stories and events in history have revealed both natures of God. God must deal with the rebellion of all the living creations he made. He gave them all (both angels and humans) the ability to choose to have a relationship with Him or not. While all of us now on earth have free will, there is no free will for anyone in hell. There is no longer a will and no longer a way. The old saying of "where there is a will, there is a way" is forever lost in hell as there is no way out of this horrific place of torment.

Many of the scriptures reveals the fate of those who wanted no part of God, his love, nor the love of his children, his prophets, and his apostles. Much sacrifice from God and his followers has been made for the sake of saving just one more soul from the pit of darkness. Yet there will come an end to all of this spiritual warfare as God will someday soon stand up from his throne and say to his Son, "Son, go get all of my faithful children and bring them home."

The Son of God will then come in the clouds of glory, and just as the days in Israel, a trumpet shall sound for the assembly of faithful believers. Those in the grave shall gather first with a new body that is immortal and will be followed by those living as the last trumpet sounds. The first blast is for the assembly. The last trumpet blast is to move out, and this will happen in the twinkling of an eye; we will be with our Lord as we meet him in the air:

> **For the Lord himself shall descend from heaven with a shout, with the voice of the archangel, and with the trump of God: and the dead in Christ shall rise first: Then we which are alive and remain shall be caught up**

**together with them in the clouds, to meet the Lord in the air: and so shall we ever be with the Lord.** (1 Thessalonians 4:16–17)

So much controversy exists in the church as to when this departure takes place as the Geneva Bible clearly states this is a departure by the participants (the true church). The King James says we will be caught up in the air.

However, instead of arguing the point, I will say this, we are the true bride of Christ. We have an intimate relationship with our groom. He has been anxiously awaiting this day for over two thousand years, and so have we, the bride of Christ. Yet, his Father sets the date for the wedding. The betrothal period for the true and faithful bride will then be over. The location for the wedding and marriage supper for the bride is in heaven as our place has been prepared for us at our Father's house. Jesus said before his ascension that "he goes to prepare a place for us that where he is, that we may be there also" (John 14:2). The wedding and the wedding supper awaits the faithful bride in heaven. There is a distinct difference between the marriage of Christ and the faithful church and the renewal of the marriage between God and Israel (and Judah).

> "**Behold, the days come, saith the LORD, that I will make a new covenant with the house of Israel, and with the house of Judah: not according to the covenant that I made with their fathers in the day that I took them by the hand to bring them out of the land of Egypt; which my covenant they brake, although I was a husband unto them, saith the LORD.**"
> Jeremiah 31:31–32 KJV

> **And I will betroth thee unto me forever.**
> Hosea 2:19

There will be another feast during the millennial reign of Christ as the celebration continues with the renewed marriage between God and Israel. Remember, there will be friends and guests at both celebrations. It will be a blessing to be included as a wedding guest or friend at either event as believers throughout the ages will be included at both celebrations. While the rewards will vary among the believers (as there are many crowns described in the Bible), we will all be in the family of God. The bride of Christ has no place to be but in heaven during the tribulation period. To place the bride in the great tribulation minimizes the intimate relationship between Christ and the faithful church. Any earthly groom and father would not test the bride by casting her into great persecution and call her up for a wedding and reception. It just doesn't make sense. It also doesn't make sense to have a heated debate over this event as the church just needs to watch for him and gather more souls into the fold. Satan would most surely want God's children not to be concerned about any wedding nor the groom to come. While Christ's admonition to "watch and be ready" has been there for all of us since his ascension, Satan's theme has always been to "get all you can while you can as it will be a while before this guy returns, if he returns at all." Satan has created innumerable ways to divide the brethren throughout the ages, and this book will not aid his cause. As for me and my house, we will seek the Lord and his return, first. All you have to do is the same, my friend. Our groom is in heaven, and our chambers are made ready as he awaits his father's command. Christ is so anxious to come after his bride!

Have you ever considered all that will occur in heaven and earth as God's judgment begins during the tribulation? The bride has to be welcomed. This will be a reunion like none other. The bride needs to be present when the seals are broken. The bride plays a role in the unsealing of the seals which starts the tribulation period. The Father and Son want the blessings of the bride to begin this judgment on earth. It must be understood that we are not needed to be there to make this happen, yet the Lamb wants us there. Neither the Son nor the Father will enjoy this opening of judgment as the magnitude of it can never be comprehended. The devastation and horror will be unbearable to most of the inhabitants of the earth. Yet, both know it has to be done to restore both heaven and the earth. Remember, the perfect will of God is that all mankind will be saved. The bride will have many loved ones left on earth: some being saved and martyred, and some unfortunately still refusing the hand of God. Yet, the prayers of the saints will play dear to the heart of God (Revelation 5:8–14). Also, the bride will have to be rewarded. It is a reward to be given to those watching and waiting for the groom. I would encourage all to be included in that number in heaven, praying rather than being one left on earth as recipients of those prayers. One must take heed to the warnings Christ gave to each of us. Christ says to watch for him. Christ said he would take one and not the other. Christ said those who keep his word would be safe, as in the Church of Philadelphia. Christ said to pray to be worthy to escape all these things (great tribulation) in Luke 21. Christ said Lot and Noah were special and were preserved from wrath, he also said his own was special to him and the Father (John 17:2–26). Paul stated that we are not children of wrath. It should be noted in chapters 4 and 5 of 1 Thessalonians, Paul also instructs us to not quench the Holy Spirit, to be sober, to be watching, to study the Word of God, to abstain from the appearance of evil, to be thankful, to not render evil for evil, to comfort those in need, not to be unruly, to work hard for a living, to put on the breastplate of faith, love and helmet of salvation, to not be caught up in fornication, and to have faith in Christ as *we* watch for Christ to return. Be a part of the *we*! He is saying brethren, be sober, and watch (1 Thessalonians 5:6).

The bride will have to be instructed and informed. Maps of the earth will be laid out in heaven as many will be appointed to rule throughout the kingdom. The Groom will reveal to us things that he has reserved only for us on that special day. Our sanctification is now complete as we prepare to follow Christ to earth as he returns in great glory. The bride has to be married and have a marriage supper, the marriage supper of the Lamb. The bride will be assigned a white horse. Not only has Christ made a place for us in the new city, he also has designated a white horse for each of us to follow Him in His glorious return. This will be the second coming of Christ to the earth where

He will reign for all eternity. Christ wants us to share in his glory. You see, just as we have been ridiculed, persecuted, slandered, beaten, starved, and martyred for over two thousand years, these things have not gone unnoticed by our Groom. Just as we have suffered with him, he desires us to share in his glorious return upon this earth (Jude 1:14; 1 Peter 4:13). Just as Christ's entry into Jerusalem was the epitome of meekness and humility, his return will likewise be in great majesty and glory. It will be an awesome and long awaited event to many, yet a dreadful and terrifying event for others. What a glorious event it will be partake in His glorious return! I cannot emphasize enough how special and spectacular this event will be to the Father, the King of kings, the faithful bride, the heavenly host and to those witnessing his return on earth. All the grand finales of our earthly fireworks celebrations combined could never match this *grand finale from heaven.* This, my friend, will be the greatest show on earth and a display that will be unrivaled by any event in the past or present. Hollywood could never come close to making something so magnificent and glorious as the return of Christ. I encourage you and plead with you to be riding *behind* the King of kings, not *under* the hooves of his white horse. Being *behind* him on earth now will get you behind him in heaven as he prepares for battle. Getting yourself a white horse is just one of the many rewards the faithful will receive after the rapture. Ride the clouds of glory up and your white horse back behind the King. What a ride to look forward to! (Acts 1:9–11, Revelation 19:14)

When it comes to defining one another's position with God, man again treads into water he should never enter. As mentioned earlier, true mature Christians will support their brothers and sisters when they stumble. As our pastor has told us in church that "he doesn't want to know all about our garbage as he has enough of his own to deal with," one has to admire his honesty, yet not to be critical of him for his truthfulness. I can relate to his message as I am far from perfect and need forgiveness daily. I must make a confession to my readers as I have said earlier that "this book is not so much for my behalf, but for yours." I must confess that going into the deeper waters where God led me during this writing experience has given me some much-needed strength which I personally needed. Christ must increase in my life, and I must decrease. Some brothers and sisters may stumble a bit, some may fall big-time, and nothing pleases Christ more than for their brothers and sisters to pick them up as he would do. The door of a man's house must be opened to our Lord for us to have the relationship he desires, and that position is between the Lord and the servant. This door is more than the heart of man; it is His entire body, soul, and spirit. As Christ calls us to open the door, it is up to us to allow Him to come in and sup with Him. Religion has a long list of works, traditions, and rituals as requirements for qualification, yet Christianity involves a relationship with the Son of God, his Father, and his Spirit. We must be proactive to pursue this relationship. Take heed of this difference and don't be ignorant of the deception of religion. All those following the false religions of the world will someday realize that Satan has craftfully used them throughout history to distort the truth, promises, and sovereignty of God. These delusions and deceptions have led them to follow other gods and other ways of salvation which kept them in the sea of darkness, facedown. Yet, many ultimately will worship Satan directly in the last days. This realization will become reality during the tribulation where many traditions and beliefs will have to be forfeited to worship the antichrist. This demand will come from none other than the dragon himself, Satan. He will have his day on stage here on planet earth, but it will not last long. So when you hear the true Savior of the world knocking at your door, for goodness sake, let him in!

> **Behold, I stand at the door and knock: if any man hear my voice, and open the door, I will come in to him, and sup with him, and he with me.** (Revelation 3:20)

This scripture is, again, some of the last words Jesus gave us while the apostle John wrote the book of Revelation on the Isle of Patmos. One particular thread goes through all the strengths mentioned, and that is *the love* one has for Christ. It is apparent from the first church mentioned that Christ knows in an instant those who truly love Him. Just take a moment to look at the very first church he addresses in Revelation:

> **Nevertheless I have somewhat against thee, because thou hast left thy first love. Remember therefore from whence thou art fallen, and repent, and do the first works, or else I will come unto thee quickly, and remove thy candlestick out of his place, except thou repent.** (Revelation 2:4–5)

As all the eleven apostles loved Jesus, the apostle John had a deep love for him, and it was evident as his letters reveal. Peter, James, and John all seemed to show a deeper love for Christ while he was with them. Our degree of faith is closely related to our love for him. The more deeply you love Jesus, the deeper your faith becomes. Jesus not only knows our love for him, he searches for such individuals that are devoted to him:

> **I am he which searcheth the reins and hearts: and I will give unto every one of you according to your works.** (Revelation 2:23)

If we deeply love him, we will love his appearing as Paul told us. If we love his appearing, then our life (works) will be a result of such love and faith as we watch and yearn for his return.

> **If therefore thou shalt not watch, I will come on the as a thief, and thou shalt not know what hour I will come upon thee.** (Revelation 3:3)

One would only have to go to hell to truly understand the love Christ has for us. Those who love him deeply truly see the eternal anguish, the suffering, the hopelessness, the deep regret, the misery, the despair and the crying that exists there. The tormented souls in hell now realize the degree of love that Christ had for them, yet they neglected his call. To love him deeply is to truly know how deep of a mess we are in here on planet earth without *him*. Also, to love him deeply is to see him being beaten, ridiculed over and over, mocked, spit upon, and nails—driven into his hands and feet—to die a horrific death…for you and me. For those who cannot understand why we suffer as Christians, try to understand *his* great sufferings, betrayal, and neglect while being the Son of the true living God. Close your eyes for just a moment. Look up on that mountain and see the cross… Look closer and see this beautiful Son of God in such a horrible and bloody condition. How can you *not* love this man? How can you look into the depths of hell and then to the cross on that mountain and not see his love for you? How can you not love a Savior bestowing so much compassion for every soul on earth? He was wounded for our transgressions and bruised for our iniquities, and by his stripes, are we healed (Isaiah 53:5). Christ made the ultimate sacrifice and did all that he could possibly do to keep you out of hell. There is no greater love to bestow upon humanity than a man to give his life for his friend. My goodness, bathe yourself in this love he has given us! You see, much was given because much was required by the Father. All the sin of humanity was put on the Son of God. The millions upon millions of animals sacrificed in the past simply came up short as man committed one more sin after another, requiring more sacrifices to be offered to the Father. The true and faithful Messiah has come and paid the ultimate price for all those who believe in him and his finished work. The true "Anointed One" did his part as he loved you as much as our Father did. Now much love is required from us to God. That is all God is looking for in us, and that is for us to think upon his name and to *truly love* him.

> **For I desire mercy, not sacrifice, and the knowledge of God more than burnt offerings.**
> (Hosea 6:6)

It is impossible to please the Father without faith. It is impossible to have faith without love. It is impossible to have faith and love and not have works (actions that reveal our faith, trust, and love for

God). The degree of faith we have is, again, directly related to how devoted we are to him. This is by no private interpretation as Christ makes this perfectly clear if you study his word.

> **For in Jesus Christ neither circumcision availeth any thing, nor uncircumcision, but faith which worketh by love.** (Galatians 5:6)

> **Hearken, my beloved brethren, Hath not God chosen the poor of this world rich in faith, and heirs of the kingdom which he hath promised to them that love him?** (James 2:5)

> **And this is his commandment, That we should believe on the name of his Son Jesus Christ, and love one another, as he gave us commandment. And he that keepeth his commandments dwelleth in him, an he in him. And herby we know that he abideth in us, by the Spirit which he hath given us.** (I John 3:23–24)

> **But without faith it is impossible to please him: for he that cometh to God must believe that he is, and that he is a rewarder of them that diligently seek him.** (Hebrews 11:6)

Never assume everyone saved gets rewarded the same as we have already discussed. Israel disobeyed the Father greatly, and their discipline from God was tremendous and overwhelming. The Jews were sent from their homeland to all ends of the earth as their rebellion and disobedience infuriated God. Yet God said he would end his time of chastisement and we are just now beginning to see this relationship beginning to be restored. The nation of Israel is back as God most certainly hasn't forgotten the chosen people of Israel.

Yes, divorce happened between the Father and Israel, and the scriptures are clear Israel will be reunited with the Father. With this thought in mind, you should take heed some of the last words Jesus said to the church:

> I come as a thief. (Revelation 16:15)
> I come quickly. (Revelation 22:20)
> Watch. (Revelation 3:3)
> I come at an hour you thinketh not. (Revelation 3:3)
> Overcome. (Revelation chapters 2 and 3)
> I Chasten my own. (Revelation 3:19)
> Let none take away your crown of glory. (Revelation 3:11)
> I will remove your candlestick. (Revelation 2:5)

Revelation could possibly be the most important book of the Bible, *especially* during the time in which we are living. There is a reason why Satan encourages mankind not to study it or says the prophecies therein have already occurred. Nothing, I assure you, has happened like is coming during the great tribulation. We are now living in the times the angel revealed to Daniel that would exist before the seventieth week of Daniel's begins. That time is now as it is a time when knowledge is greatly increasing, and people are definitely moving to and fro. You can now take a ride into space if you have enough funds to do so! Yet as our knowledge has increased, so has the deception that surrounds the four corners of the earth. This deception will get even greater and will lead multitudes upon multitudes into the great tribulation. Seek the Lord now while he may be found.

> **Serve the Lord with fear, and rejoice with trembling. Kiss the Son, lest he be angry, and ye perish from the way, when his wrath is kindled but a little while. Blessed are they that put their trust in him.** (Psalms 2:11–12)

Finally, we see the church mentioned again in Revelation 22:16–17 as Christ makes one more invitation, though this time he includes the bride in his invitation, to "come" as well. It was his way of telling all that his bride's desire is his desire and that is for all to come, as the water of life is there for those who have been freed by his grace, forever. I have had a deep conviction, to say the least, to awaken those being asleep concerning the departure of the church (rapture, taken, or catching away). While many will mock this discussion and some may be offended to some degree, it will hopefully lead many to consider where they actually stand in the kingdom of heaven. I do not apologize for continually beating this drum as it is my prayer that the drum's sound may open some deafened ears to the trumpet sound that could come at any moment. Jesus makes it very clear that His sheep hear His voice. We will now move on in to the journey as we focus on Babylon.

This journey mentions the fall of Babylon and it is very important for all to understand how this is not just a city but a metaphor for the established evil government led by the unholy trinity that will rule during the latter days. It shall fall never to rise again. It should be noted that there will be great rejoicing made in heaven when this Babylonian Empire is finally destroyed. Much speculation has been made as to where this city is located, and all I can say is that you don't want to go there. You don't want to be a participant to the evil empire it represents. Babylon is the world system of power, wealth, suppressing the poor, and hating and countering the Word of God and all authorities. This system will lead to a world government and domination as Satan desires to rule and reign here on earth. There will come a day that no man may be able to buy food, medicine, or anything without being loyal to this satanic beast. I would caution *every* soul on earth *not* to take his mark upon the hand or forehead. The number of the beast has been foretold and is 666.

There are spiritual strongholds that have taken over many cities, and these cities are harboring demonic spirits and have for many years. We can see it clearly, and it seems the corruption and violence is getting worse and worse in our cities. There are so many good people in these cities, and we should pray for their safety as violence and chaos is putting many lives in the constant state of fear.

The city of the great Babylon of the latter times has not yet been revealed though there are many scholarly opinions of where this city could be. However, we certainly do not know at this point in time. This city that has represented so much evil and been responsible for so much bloodshed will utterly be destroyed as foretold in Revelation 18.

Even so, come, Lord Jesus.

# Chapter 18

---

# A Journey in the Book of Jeremiah: The Fall of Jerusalem

> Then said Jeremiah unto them, Thus shall ye say to Zedekiah: Thus saith the LORD God of Israel; Behold, I will turn back the weapons of war that are in your hands, wherewith ye fight against the king of Babylon, and against the Chaldeans, which besiege you without the walls, and I will assemble them into the midst of this city.

Throughout history, many countries and civilizations have attempted to annihilate the Jewish people and the nation of Israel. The Israel Defense Forces are now preparing for attacks on six different fronts as they are aware of their past and are doing their best to prepare for the worst. More attacks will be inevitable; however, Israel and Jerusalem shall never cease to exist. They will last forever and ever. We have already discussed how archeology has proven the history not only of Israel but actually the history of mankind. The Holy Land is holy because it was and will be the dwelling place of a Holy God.

> Sing and rejoice, O daughter of Zion: for, lo, I come, and I will dwell in the midst of thee, saith the Lord. (Zechariah 2:10)

> **Thus saith the Lord; I am returned unto Zion, and will dwell in the midst of Jerusalem: and Jerusalem shall be called the city of truth, and the mountain of the Lord of hosts the holy mountain.** (Zechariah 8:3)

> **And I will make her that halted a remnant, and her that was cast far off a strong nation: and the Lord shall reign over them in mount Zion from henceforth, even for ever.** (Micah 4:7)

While we observe the mountains and valleys that Israel has endured throughout history, we see here in this journey where the message being delivered was one that no one in Israel wanted to hear from the prophet Jeremiah. Jeremiah was a special prophet of God as He chose him as a vessel for His message before Jeremiah was even born. This message to King Zedekiah was that because Israel had abandoned God, offered sacrifices to false gods, and made idols of other gods, the Holy City would be utterly destroyed. To whom much is given, much is required (Luke 12:48). Take heed America.

God had told Jeremiah that his message would not be a popular one as he soon discovered. The priests, citizens, nor the king wanted to hear such a message, yet God gave His prophet strength and courage to continue boldly in proclaiming the judgment to come.

This closely mirrors the attitude of the world today. Many church doors are being closed, and many pastors have resigned or have been dismissed for the very same reason. It's an unfortunate repetition of history but on a global scale as judgment is coming to the entire world. For both Israel and then the inhabitants of the world today, we see a failure to honor God. The pursuit of power, fame, fortune, and pleasure leaves no room, no need, and no thought of the Creator of all things. It is a trap set by Satan. The lust of the flesh jumps in only to be caught in the sharp teeth of the trap. There are two people that this journey mentions, and one of a king and one of a prophet. King Zedekiah would be the last king of Judah, and Jerusalem would soon be surrounded by the huge army sent by Nebuchadnezzar from Babylon. It would be some six hundred years later that another King would enter the gates of Jerusalem, though not in all of his glory. Jesus entered the eastern gate of Jerusalem on a donkey, and while the gate is closed to this day, the hope of Israel is that the gate will remain closed until the Messiah comes.

It is so unfortunate that the Jewish people didn't accept him while he was here, but they most certainly will acknowledge that failure when he comes again.

> **And then shall appear the sign of the Son of man in heaven: and then shall all the tribes of the earth mourn, and they shall see the Son of man coming in the clouds of heaven with power and great glory.** (Matthew 24:30)

> **And they shall look upon me whom they have pierced, and they shall mourn for him, as one that is in bitterness for his firstborn.** (Zechariah 12:10)

> **And one shall say unto him, "What are these wounds in thine hands?" Then he shall answer, "Those with which I was wounded in the house of my friends."** (Zechariah 13:5)

In the future, Jerusalem will once again be surrounded by the enemies of God just as we see in this journey. Jesus Christ, the man who was ridiculed, beaten beyond recognition, had nails driven into precious His hands and feet, and who was hung on a cross will be the one who comes to defeat these enemies of God. It will be both moving and heartbreaking to witness the sorrow of the Jewish people as they see the scars on the Savior who saves them. The Jewish people, as well as many persecuted believers, will be more than ready for the Prince of Peace to return. They will joyfully sing a song they used to sing in the streets of Jerusalem.

"Blessed is he who comes in the name of the Lord" (Psalm 118:10–26, Matthew 23:39).

This future scene also brings to mind all those in the Great White Throne Judgment that will come after the great tribulation. Those in this judgment will give account for all the sin, all the evil, and lustful deeds done on earth. They will see these nail-scarred hands as Jesus opens the Book of Life and the books of their works. I implore you, my friend, to abandon whatever is in your life keeping you destined to this fateful judgment. I assure you, it will happen to all who have neglected, refused, and mocked the salvation of God. There is a reason why the healed wounds in the Son of God is still visible. One is to show the tribes of Israel and all who will face Christ in judgment that He was the risen Son of God and Savior of the world. He was, and is, and will forever be the Messiah. Jesus was perfect and died a perfect man, yet he was God in the flesh. God the Father, God the Son, and God the Holy Spirit, while all separate beings, are one in essence. While Jesus descended to Hell and took the keys of death and Hell, his healed wounds were still visible after he appeared to his disciples.

**Jesus saith unto him, "Thomas, because thou hast seen me, thou hast believed; blessed are they that have not seen, and yet have believed."** (John 20:29)

Thomas had heard that Jesus had risen from the dead, yet he was stubborn and told the other disciples that he would not believe them until he saw the wounds in the Son of God himself. While many people point to the fault of Thomas, they fail to realize the faithful commitment Thomas made to Christ after this and was later martyred for his faith in Christ. While living on this new earth one billion years from now, we will still observe the scars on our Savior, forever reminding us of the tremendous sacrifice and cost it took to *get* and *keep* us on the beautiful new earth.

Let us return to our journey in Jerusalem, and we see an impending invasion from Babylon, and while the prophet Jeremiah is hated and despised by all, he still tells all that they will be taken captive into Babylon, and the city and temple will be destroyed. Jeremiah was deeply troubled by this revelation and the impending doom of Judah. He was known as the weeping prophet as he not only loved God, he also loved God's people. We should all pray for God's people and for peace in Jerusalem. If you deeply love God our Father, you will deeply love the Jews and Israel.

The days of King Zedekiah as king were coming to an end, and there will be no king until Jesus returns in all His glory. King Zedekiah was stubborn and never heeded God's warning from his prophet, and even though the king tried to escape, he was caught by the Babylonian Army. All of the king's sons were all killed as he watched, and then his eyes were gouged out just after they were killed. This was a sad ending for Judah and Jerusalem who thought they were invincible, but were defeated in a mighty way. These folks thought they were protected as they had been for years, yet their sinful acts against God caught up with them.

The worship of false gods, the idolatry, and the failure to overcome these faults ultimately put them over the edge with God. Jesus would not arrive for another six hundred years, yet when He did, He came humbly as one could. Yet, many would never accept this King as they wanted a king to deliver them from the Roman rule and power and dominion over the entire land. He was then wounded for all our transgressions, both the Jews and the Gentiles, and through his stripes, through his healed hands, feet, and side are we healed and healed indefinitely. While Jerusalem is preparing for another assault from their enemies, Christians have no fear and possess the inner peace and security that indwells in our soul and spirit. The victory has been won, and though the armies of Satan encircle us, we shall not be moved as our armor is the Word of God and the finished work of his Son. (Ephesians 6)

This journey takes us to a king and a prophet as they both represent the world today: one is proclaiming the truth and judgment that is soon to come unless true repentance is made; two, a king and people who are totally blinded by the cares and pleasures of this world. It is my prayer that you take heed, my friend, and open your ears and your eyes to the wisdom of God. While all the prophets are now in heaven, their messages are resonating to the faithful servants as we now are witnessing many of the signs they once prophesied of.

There is nothing new under the sun, as this story resembles a similar one to come in the future. Listen to the words of the prophet and do not fall into the clutches of Satan, as this king and the tribe of Judah did some six hundred years BC.

# CHAPTER 19

## A Journey in the Book of Ezekiel: In a Nutshell

**Notwithstanding the children rebelled against me: they walked not in my statutes, neither kept my judgments to do them, which if a man do, he shall even live in them; they polluted my sabbaths: then I said, I would pour out my fury upon them, to accomplish my anger against them in the wilderness. Nevertheless I withdrew mine hand, and wrought for my name's sake, that it should not be polluted in the sight of the heathen, in whose sight I brought them forth.**

There is perhaps no better place to sum up the journeys in the Old Testament than right here in Ezekiel 20:21–22. The book of Ezekiel highlights the demise of Israel, the future conflicts of Israel and the restoration and hope of Israel. In this particular journey, we have to go to this place in time and see why these judgements came to pass. It appears the leaders wanted Ezekiel to inquire on just what God's intentions were now that Jerusalem was overtaken by the Babylonians as they were now in captivity. God is not amused by their inquiry as he quickly reminds them of their past. Ezekiel is addressing the few left in Jerusalem as well as all of those now kept captive in Babylon. Remember, while Christians are defined as brothers, sisters, and friends of Christ, we are collectively called his bride and his church. Likewise, God's relationship to Israel was defined as his friends and children individually, yet collectively, they were the bride of the Father once divorced, but soon to be reunited after the Great Tribulation. All these close relationships are desperately being utilized by God to define an even more intimate relationship that exists when we take his hand in faith and believe in him. You, my friend, are the apple of his eye and very special to our Creator and his Son.

God speaks of Israel's rebellion, and he is referring to *his children*. The mere fact that God still calls them his children shows his great love for these people. "My children have rebelled against me". God's heart is torn as He had chosen these people through the family of Abraham, Isaac, and Jacob to represent him and to reveal himself through this nation of Israel. If you have ever been a parent, you are very much aware of how a child can be rebellious. Yet we still love them, and without correction, they will not know the consequences of their error. This was so true as we recognize the level of rebellion Israel had toward God. Did all of Israel rebel against God? No, as Caleb and Joshua were the only two who had faith in God that they could take the Promised Land and conquer the enemies therein. Yet, a rebellion against them stirred the hearts of everyone, and Caleb and Joshua were overruled by the majority.

This was just one example of the numerous times the Israelites rebelled against God. God also says that they "walked not in my statutes" as described in verse 21. God was telling Ezekiel that he had given his rules and his law to them not only to abide by but to tell those in their path of these truths. This message is to be proclaimed even to this day. God the Father and God the Son and God the Holy Spirit must be shown to the world through those who are abiding in Christ Jesus. Yes, we yearn for the day when we will see the face of the Father and the Son here on this beautiful planet. It was the nation of Israel first to represent God, and they still do. The church is the bride of Christ. Israel is the bride of the Father, and they will be reconciled (Ezekiel 16:8, Hosea 14:4).

Yet, the light of the world and the completion of the Jewish faith rests on the finished work of the Messiah. We all need to be a Jew—a completed Jew. Jesus Christ fulfilled the law, and his sacrifice created a better law, the law of his grace. All of the journeys in the Old Testament have shown the true nature of God, and it is one of purity and utmost of holiness. We, at our very best behavior, are still as filthy rags as compared to God's purity and righteousness. God has not abandoned his people as some have believed. The nation and people of Israel have been blinded by so much, yet the final days or the last days (great tribulation) will be a time when their eyes and ears will be opened. Israel will again be surrounded by her enemies, and while it seems all hope is lost, the King of kings will appear in great glory and with millions of saints and angels following him (Jude 1:14) (Revelation 19:14).

So we go back to the time of this journey, and we must listen carefully to what God is telling Israel. Needless to say, God is not pleased with these folks as he allows the Babylonian Army to take his people captive.

Israel was the nation chosen to represent God. Therefore, they had to know him and his laws to be able to truly represent him. To know the rules and to walk in them was the intent. Israel could not keep the idols of their past out of their minds as they strayed in their walk to the point of God destroying them all. Yet, God had mercy on them and did not destroy His people. The people murmured not only against Moses and Aaron but against God as well. The nation forgot the agony of being under Egyptian bondage for four hundred years as they complained day after day. They enjoyed the label of being God's chosen, yet they chose several times to walk in the ways of the Egyptian gods and idols as they neglected him. Even after they were delivered into the Promised Land (those youth who did not perish in the desert), they had periods of falling back into idolatry, as we discussed in the days of the kings and judges. Now we see God's chosen again in bondage just as their ancestors were in Egypt.

God was reminding Israel why they were in the position they were in. While God is patient and merciful, rest assured He will discipline His children. They rebelled against God, then they walked in ways that dishonored God and his laws. They literally turned their backs on the one who had chosen them, delivered them, and provided for them a land flowing with milk and honey. All they had to do was to honor him and his ways. We all need to take heed of their history, and if you read the entire book of Ezekiel, you will find that

God will remember his people. God says he will call his people back to their homeland, and he has. God says he will be their God, and they will be his sons and daughters, and this will happen.

Yet the enemy of Israel still lingers today. The enemy that is relentless and seeking whom he can devour. The same enemy that drew them away from the Father in their early history. The enemy is devising plans to persecute and utterly destroy the Jewish people. Now while they appear to be safely settled in their homeland, there are trials, tribulation, persecution, deliverance and judgement on the horizon for Israel and the inhabitants of the earth.

While Israel will be delivered at the end of the tribulation, the faithful church will be delivered to the gates of heaven before the "day of the Lord" begins. Those living believers as well as those in the grave will be rewarded with immortal bodies to forever be with God. That, my friend, is the deliverance you want to be a part of! Call it rapture, call it departure, call it caught up, call it anything you want, but don't call me, I'll be gone. Those in the past and those now living most certainly haven't been exempt from trials, tribulation, and persecution. Again we as true followers of God are not popular in this world we are living today.

*Great* tribulation is coming. Great persecution is coming. Great trials are coming. As the world will soon see, the judgment will be absolutely terrifying for the earth and her inhabitants. Scared? You should be if you are left here after Jesus takes his faithful bride to heaven. Encouraged? I am with you. Concerned? We all should be. Concerned for those who are not ready to be in the "Delivered" column of the Book of Life. Yes, many during the great tribulation will be delivered only after they have been persecuted and most likely martyred for their faith in God.

Why are we discussing this again? If you have seen topics and journeys repeating the same message, then you should take heed as the message being discussed is obviously an important one. We see in this journey also that the Sabbaths have been polluted, and to remember the Sabbath is to remember God. Not only who he is but just what all he has done. It is an impressive résumé. We should remember God by attending a local assembly as the Scripture instructs us to not forsake the assembling of the church. We are part of the body of Christ, and we all have gifts that build a unity and effective mission to the local community as well as supporting missions throughout the world. Whether your gift is singing, teaching, or cleaning, it is important to be a part in the local church. We are so blessed to have our pastors in the churches today. Our pastors are under a great deal of stress, and we need to pray fully and financially support them now more than ever. The more you care about Jesus, the more you care about others. There are a lot of others out there who are under a tremendous amount of stress. This pandemic has placed additional stress on our church and pastors. We should not neglect to support our church and pastor financially, as many churches are now in financial trouble due to lack of giving and attendance. They are called men of God, and they should not have to worry about their personal finances on top of everything else going on. I have filled in for pastors in the past, and you cannot imagine the work and preparation required to give just a single message. Yet most pastors have well over 150 of these messages to prepare for the flock year in and year out. It is a tremendous responsibility to be feeding and caring for the flock. Just remember, he is the shepherd, and he is the *leader* of the flock. Too many folks forget this and try to meddle in the pastor's role in leading the flock. While there are specific responsibilities for the elders, deacons, and teachers, remember the pastor has been called to lead the church in preparation for the Chief Shepherd's return.

> **And when the chief Shepherd shall appear, ye shall receive a crown of glory that fadeth not away.** (1 Peter 5:4)

I memorized the twenty-third Psalm when I was a child. I encourage you to do the same and meditate on it when times get tough:

> **The Lord is my shepherd; I shall not want. He maketh me to lie down in green pastures: he leadeth me beside the still waters. He restoreth my soul: he leadeth me in the**

**paths of righteousness for his name's sake. Yea, though I walk through the valley of the shadow of death, I will fear no evil: for thou art with me; thy rod and thy staff, they comfort me. Thou preparest a table before me in the presence of mine enemies: thy anointest my head with oil; my cup runneth over. Surely goodness and mercy shall follow me all of the days of my life, and I will dwell in the house of the Lord forever.** (Psalm 23)

Remember the Sabbath and keep it holy, and by doing so, you show honor to God.

Now as we conclude these very important journeys in the Old Testament, the New Testament will involve five journeys that are that are found in chapter 20. It is amazing how these have all fit together to complete the message of this book. The verses of all five of these will be printed, and these journey(s) will take you from Matthew to Revelation.

So we thank our Father for all the wisdom that he has given us on these journeys in the Old Testament. Please search and study these precious books as it reveals the master plan of God. Now I pray we pay very close attention to these last journeys as we go to five different locations. Jesus Christ has now come to the earth, and these intriguing moments in time are coming to life again.

# Chapter 20

# Five Journeys in the New Testament

*Journey in Matthew*

> And He said unto her, "What wilt thou?" She saith unto Him, "Grant that these my two sons may sit, the one on thy right hand, and the other on the left, in thy kingdom." But Jesus answered and said, "Ye know not what ye ask. Are ye able to drink of the cup that I shall drink of, and to be baptized with the baptism that I am baptized with? They say unto Him, "We are able."

*Journey in Luke*

> And they asked Him, saying, "Master, we know that thou sayest and teachest rightly, neither acceptest thou the person of any, but teachest the way of God truly: Is it lawful for us to give tribute unto Cæsar, or no?"

*Journey in John*

> Then said Jesus to them again, "Peace be unto you: as my Father hath sent me, even so send I you." And when He had said this, He breathed on them, and saith unto them, "Receive ye the Holy Ghost."

*Journey in Acts*

> Testifying both to the Jews, and also to the Greeks, repentance toward God, and faith toward our Lord Jesus Christ. And now, behold, I go bound in the spirit unto Jerusalem, not knowing the things that shall befall me there.

*Journey in Revelation*

> And he said unto me, "It is done. I am Alpha and Omega, the beginning and the end. I will give unto him that is athirst of the fountain of the water of life freely. He that overcometh shall inherit all things; and I will be his God, and he shall be my son."

Peace. Isn't it what we truly and deeply desire? As again, we look forward into eternity, we see a place so full of peace, yet there is another place where peace never has existed, nor will ever exist in the depths of hell. There are several reasons why there is peace in heaven and one is that God the Father is there, and the second is that his Son also is there. Peace is internal as well as external. The reason we do not externally see peace on earth is because the majority of those on earth have no internal peace. There is no rioting in heaven nor will there be on the new earth. There is no murdering in heaven nor will there be on the new earth. There is no stealing in heaven nor will there be anything taken on the new earth. There is no racism in heaven nor will there be on the new earth. There is no persecution in heaven, nor will there be on the new earth. There is no pain in heaven, nor will there be any on the new earth.

The internal peace that I had when facing death in that coal mine cannot be described, yet it was there. The mountain was coming down on top of me in that dark coal mine near Buckhannon, West Virginia, yet there was no fear, no unknowns, nothing but peace. I assure you that all other religions may try to sell their own peace, but it is not real and is counterfeit. You cannot purchase it, nor can you earn it. It is a mere result of placing your trust in the finished work of Jesus Christ. Just why is over two-thirds of the Bible (and most of this book) focusing on the Old Testament? The answer is simple and it is to show us mere humans just how much trouble we are truly in on this planet. Our position with God is dire, to say the least. Then the focus turns to our need of a Savior to redeem us from this tremendous debt. A debt we could never pay. While the first two-thirds of the Bible lays the foundation of heaven and earth, it also lays the foundation of our salvation. We now will see a babe wrapped in swaddling clothes coming to the earth. He has come to wrap us in fine white linen, as our filthy rags may be cleansed through his righteousness.

While many will receive white robes in heaven, others will receive the fine white linen, and those will be in that number following Christ back to earth (Revelation 19).

*Matthew*

> **And He said unto her, "What wilt thou?" She saith unto Him, "Grant that these my two sons may sit, the one on thy right hand, and the other on the left, in thy kingdom." But Jesus answered and said, "Ye know not what ye ask. Are ye able to drink of the cup that I shall drink of, and to be baptized with the baptism that I am baptized with?" They say unto Him, "We are able." (Matthew 20:21–22 KJV)**

The twenty-first and twenty-second verse after chapter 20 in Matthew takes us to where the mother of James and John was seeking a place for her sons when Christ sits on his throne. Jesus tells her that she doesn't know just what she is asking for.

The cup Jesus was about to take was the cup of wrath from the Father that all of humanity was responsible for. It was the remedy for our sin that only the pure sacrifice of the Son of God could offer. No man could possibly be eligible for such a position to drink this cup, regardless of his status with God.

It would be the first and only time that the Father and the Son would be separated. What a burdensome task it must have been for our Savior to endure. The mother of James and the disciples had no clue that the greatest event in all of human history was about to take place. The mercy and grace of God would soon be available to all of humanity for those who accept His beloved Son. This journey also speaks on how the other apostles were jealous of James and John as they saw the favor Christ had for them. While Jesus deeply cared for all of his disciples, he knew what lay ahead for each of them, and he knew that Peter, James, and John would be the leaders of the disciples. They loved Jesus *deeply*. There is love, and then there is deep love. We should not just love God. We should love him deeply. We should not like him; we should adore him. We should not merely accept him; we should run the race for him and grasp his hand with enthusiasm and joy.

Those called and chosen of God must choose to be faithful to Him. While rewards are given to us and most certainly appreciated, we must cherish the love and mercy that God has abundantly bestowed to His children. God said, "If you love me, you will keep my commandments." While we all know it is impossible to keep them all, it is not impossible to try. That, my friend, is the difference between truly loving God and just giving him lip service and a dollar in the plate at Christmas. One must not minimize the love Jesus had for the other disciples in this application, but focus on the fact that these two men (and Peter) were very special to Christ as they had a deep love for him.

*Luke*

**And they asked him, saying, "Master, we know that thou sayest and teachest rightly, neither acceptest thou the person of any, but teachest the way of God truly: Is it lawful for us to give tribute unto Cæsar, or no?"** (Luke 20:21–22 KJV)

As we go forward into the book of Luke, we see in the twenty-first and twenty-second verses after chapter 20. As we go into Luke Chapter 20, verses 21 and 22, we find Jesus had just told the parable of the husbandmen and the vineyard. In this parable, Jesus was referring to many of the Jews, as rejecting him and giving the vineyard to others (the Gentiles). The chief priests and scribes had conspired to take and kill Jesus, so they were plotting a way to entrap him so that he would be killed. It was just as he had told them in the parable.

The trap they were setting for Jesus didn't work as they questioned Christ whether or not to pay taxes to Caesar. Jesus quickly said a man was to pay the taxes due to Caesar, and it broke the trap. They were hoping to get Jesus to do the opposite so they could take him to the governor and charge him with a crime. There were many Jews who simply had a deep enmity toward Jesus, and this hatred was expressed many times in the New Testament. Many of the Jewish people were wanting to be freed from Roman rule rather than seeing a blind man healed. They were put in charge of the vineyard (the earth), yet they disrespected the owner and sought to kill Him. This was a parable directed to those seeking the life of Christ, and this parable only infuriated them even more. Many blame the Jews for taking the life of Christ; however, *all* of humanity is responsible for His crucifixion.

Later in AD 70, the Romans destroyed the temple, and the Jewish rebellion was ended by a huge Roman Army. Jesus had told them that the temple would be destroyed, and it was. The prophets also said that Israel would someday be restored, and it now has been restored. The tribes have been returning to the homeland since 1948.

While many Jewish people have accepted Christ as their King and Messiah (Messianic Jews), the nation of Israel is still waiting for the Messiah to arrive. This was not so for the Jewish apostles as we journey into the book of John. Our journey in the New Testament continues as we go to the twenty-second verse after Chapter 20. This great moment in time was when the apostles witness the risen Son of God appearing to them. Let us rejoice as we revisit this life-changing time in human history!

*John*

It seems appropriate that the first person to see the risen Lord was Mary Magdalene (verse 18). Women are special to God. She had met the apostles and told them of his resurrection. She was numbered among the faithful apostles who stayed by the side of Jesus and deeply loved Him. The apostles were in the upper room where they were hiding from the Jews, when Mary came to the door with the good news. The entire journey of all the scriptures has been revealed to the apostles and to all of mankind—Jesus has risen from the dead.

He and he alone gives us peace. Internal peace and external peace. He was sent by his Father, and now he was empowering those close to Him to go in His name and tell the world the good news. He is and was and will always be the Savior of the world.

The journey of peace now goes into the twenty-first verse after chapter 20 in the book of Acts, and we are now nearing the finish line in what God wants you to know in 2022.

*Acts*

> **Testifying both to the Jews, and also to the Greeks, repentance toward God, and faith toward our Lord Jesus Christ. And now, behold, I go bound in the spirit unto Jerusalem, not knowing the things that shall befall me there.** (Acts 20:21–22)

You see, my friend, the message of all of these journeys points to repentance as we discover from the beginning of these journeys that is what God is seeking: *Repentance*. True repentance is a *result* of a *genuine* confession and change of heart in accepting Jesus as Lord and Savior. Our debt has been paid by the blood of the Lamb, though we must always remember the high cost of our deliverance. It is a cost that should energize our desire to know and serve the Lord Jesus every day of our lives. Repentance is turning away from the old self and turning onto the narrow path that leads us home. The path was designed by God but was made possible by His Son for those who faithfully turn to Him. It is a narrow pathway that very few actually turn to as most of humanity choose the broad road of destruction that leads them off the cliff into the pits of hell.

These journeys are coming to an end as we visit the last book of the Bible. It is perhaps my favorite book as I have been intrigued and encouraged by it most of my life. The quoted scripture goes into the following chapter as we focus on the twenty-first and twenty-second verses after chapter 20.

> **And He said unto me, "It is done. I am Alpha and Omega, the beginning and the end. I will give unto him that is athirst of the fountain of the water of life freely. He that overcometh shall inherit all things; and I will be his God, and he shall be my son."** (Revelation 21:6–7)

Yes, my friend, it is done. For all those both in heaven and hell, it is done. For all those going to heaven and hell, it is done. For all those sitting down with the Prince of Peace at the marriage supper of the Lamb, it is done. For there are those who have taken the hand of God who may freely drink of the fountain of the water of life that comes from the throne of God on the new earth. The invitation is for all to come to the fountain that only Christ can provide, and he will give you an abundant and joyful life.

If you are a saved and faithful servant, pray for even more strength and boldness as the Spirit of God is yearning to shine forth in these last days. If you are not in the family of God, you must seek him while he may be found.

> **But if from thence thou shalt seek the Lord thy God, thou shall find him, if thou seek him with all thy heart and with all thy soul.** (Deuteronomy 4:29)

You may say this simple prayer to be in his beautiful family:

> Father, I am a sinner, and I no longer want to live in this sea of darkness. I realize now that my works cannot save me from my sin. I know that your Son, Jesus, paid the price for all of my sin. He came to this earth, born of a virgin, and died on the cross for me. I believe he arose from the dead with the keys of death and hell, and I accept your Son, Jesus, as my Lord and my Savior. I will now take your hand as you promised to lead me to green pastures and by the still waters, for you have restored my soul. I ask of these things in the name of Jesus Christ, now my Lord and Savior. Thank you, Father, for accepting me into your family. Amen
>
> If you said this prayer with your mouth and believed it in your heart, your name was just recorded in the Lamb's Book of Life. That, my friend, is priceless! **That if thou shalt confess with thy mouth the Lord Jesus, and shalt believe in thine heart that God hath raised him from the dead, thou shalt be saved.** (Romans 10:9)

Welcome home. You are now of royal blood and in the family of God. Trust in Christ as he has proven his divinity and trustworthiness. Grow in him through study and prayer as you joyfully seek him and his return. Live a life watching for him as we are nearing the last days. Now rest in the family of God as he is sovereign and in control. He has proven himself over and over since the beginning of time. He has such a wonderful plan for you now and for all eternity. My, what hope we have, being included in his wonderful family! I look so forward to being with you as we travel that narrow path together waiting for our Groom!

Please consider these two things as we near the end of this book: Many readers knowingly and unknowingly are nearing the end of their lives on this earth and must consider these two imperative points.

1-don't be deceived:

We are living in a world of great deception and Satan's greatest tool of deception is for one to think that he is "OK" with God, yet in reality he is "OK" with Satan. There are those actively worshiping Satan on earth, yet they will all abandon their loyalty to him once they enter the gates of hell. They will never forgive themselves for their ill-fated decision to choose Satan over God.

However, the pits of hell will also be filled with those that neglected a true relationship with God for their own "god" they fabricated in their minds to fit their lifestyle. A lifestyle totally committed against the will of God as he serves himself and Satan. The lifestyle becomes easier and easier as one finds a scripture or two that they brazenly claim, yet the intentions of their heart does not serve and honor God.

The second point is this:

Like it or not, you have chosen to either serve God in your life or you have chosen to serve yourself.

When you have chosen to serve Christ, you have actually chosen a vault full of rewards and gifts. You get a whole lot more than deliverance from an eternal Hell.

By choosing Christ, ***you have chosen***:

- A new immortal, glorified body that will never die. A perfect body made possible through the finished work of Jesus Christ
- To be a recipient of the inheritance of the new earth (imagine an earth more beautiful than the Garden of Eden)
- To walk with God on this earth. Just as Adam, Enoch, Noah, Abraham, and Moses did, so shall the children of God do throughout eternity
- To eternally eat and drink of the fine fruit and food that is produced on the new earth
- To take endless vacations. God created a vast universe so that his children would never become bored. Not only will we enjoy a new earth, but imagine exploring the other galaxies that our Father created
- To praise, honor, exalt, love and to better know the God of Abraham, Isaac and Jacob, and his Son, Jesus. He will be our God and we shall be his children. Forever
- To be reunited with loved ones who were dear to your heart. Imagine being with all those who prayed with you, prayed for you, cried for you, cried with you, stayed by your bedside when you were sick, stayed by your side when you were down, encouraged you while you were so depressed… and yes, you have chosen Christ who has ultimately done all the above for you

Unfortunately, most have chosen the alternative to choosing Christ which means ***you have chosen***:

- To be cast into the lake of fire in your old body. The story of the rich man and Lazarus makes it perfectly clear those in hell have a body as they yearn for even a drop of water to quench their thirst
- To be a recipient of the lake of fire forever and to never see the light of day again. The cones in your eyes will never

be needed. While you chose to be blind to God's Word on earth, you have also chosen to be blind throughout all of eternity in outer darkness

- To never walk with again with anyone as it's impossible to walk when one is confined to a pit
- To eternally starve and crave of thirst. The moisture content in the lake of fire is zero. No fresh water springs. No freshwater rivers. No freshwater lakes. Just a lake of fire. You have chosen this for your eternal home.
- To only dream of past vacations on earth, as all the beauty of God's creation can never be experienced again. The regret will be unbearable
- To curse and hate Satan, his demons, friends and self for paving the broad roadway that you had taken to the pits of hell. The blame game will never end
- To never be a part of a family gathering, or a celebration, or a fine dinner out, as it will be physically impossible in the pit.

So be as smart as an animal as all the animals that God called into the ark obeyed his voice. They chose to obey God and were rescued from his wrath. They turned when called and chose to journey to the ark of safety.

As we're nearing the end of this book, I thank the Holy Spirit of God for leading me in "What God wants you to know in 2022. It has taken countless hours to bring this book to you. It has been an honor and a privilege to serve the Lord by completing this writing. To the Father, the Son and the Spirit be the glory.

On the completion of this book, my prayer now is that I would have more of the mind of Christ, the heart of God, and the power of the Spirit to fill me as we continue on our journey home. This is the message, my friend: to be closer to our Creator and to know him more. That is my desire and hopefully your's as well.

As I write these last words, I pray the Holy Spirit surrounds and comforts you during these last days we are living. If this book helped you, please obtain another for a friend or loved one who needs the message contained in *What God Wants You to Know in 2022*. I hope it has been a help to each of you reading. There is perhaps no better scripture to complete the message of this book than Psalm 33. Enjoy.

> **Rejoice in the Lord, O ye righteous: for praise is comely for the upright. Praise the Lord with harp: sing unto him with the psaltery and an instrument of ten strings. Sing unto him a new song: play skillfully with a loud noise. For the word of the Lord is right; and all his works are done in truth. He loveth righteousness and judgement: the earth is full of the goodness of the Lord. By the word of the Lord were the heavens made, and all the host of them by the breath of his mouth. He gathereth the waters of the sea together as an heap: he layeth up the depth in storehouses. Let all the earth fear the Lord: let all the inhabitants of the world stand in awe of him. For he spake, and it was done: he commanded, and it stood fast. The Lord bringeth the counsel of the heathen to nought: he maketh the devices of the people of none effect. The counsel of the Lord standeth for ever, the thoughts of his heart to all generations. Blessed is the nation whose God is the Lord: and the people whom he hath chosen for his own inheritance. The Lord looketh from heaven: he beholdeth all the sons of men. From the place of his habitation, he looketh upon all the inhabitants of the earth. He fashioneth their hearts alike: he considereth all their works. There is no king saved by the multitude of an host: a mighty man is not delivered by much strength. An horse is a vain thing for safety: neither shall he deliver any by his great strength. Behold, the eye of the Lord is upon them that fear him,**

**upon them that hope in his mercy: To deliver their soul from death, and to keep them alive in famine. Our soul waiteth for the Lord: he is our help and our shield. For our heart shall rejoice in him, because we have trusted in his holy name. Let thy mercy, O Lord, be upon us, according as we hope in thee.**

Regardless of your standing in Christ, I just want to tell you that God loves you, my friend. May the Lord bless you and keep you. May his face shine upon you and be gracious unto you. May the Lord lift his countenance upon you and give you peace.

Even so, come, Lord Jesus!

# About the Author

Jamie Thomas was born, raised, and educated in the coal mining hills of West Virginia. He has been a child of God since the age of sixteen. Jamie considers himself a simple man who loves God with all his heart, mind, and soul.

Jamie received his bachelor's degree from Fairmont State University and became a licensed private pilot while attending college. Following college, he attended officer school and undergraduate pilot training (UPT) in the United States Air Force. Jamie realized early in UPT that God had other plans for him, and he returned to the mountains of West Virginia.

His career led him to the energy sector in West Virginia and Ohio for over thirty years. On August 12, 1996, Jamie was involved in a serious underground mining accident where the mountain suddenly collapsed upon him, burying him under four feet of rock. It was this miracle in the mountains that led to this writing some twenty-six years later.

Jamie tells the story of this miracle in the mountains as well as the miracle of his calling in this wonderful book. Jamie has served God in various ministries but has always been led to write a book. This is the humble culmination of that calling. Jamie wants to reinforce that the focus of the book is not to be upon him and his life but upon God and what God wants you to know in 2022.

CPSIA information can be obtained
at www.ICGtesting.com
Printed in the USA
JSHW080429191022
31831JS00002B/9